Where Would You Buy Your Running Shoes?

Does it make any more sense to buy a one-size-fits-all how-to-succeed book than it does to buy running shoes at a one-size-fits-all shoe store? Can a 3-, 5-, 7-, or 10-step 'one-size-fits-all' formula for success transform your life? This book explains why one-size-fits-all success books fail to significantly change you. It then teaches the principles that will allow you to succeed, to radically change what you see as possible, and to step boldly into living your dreams now. Why wait? What's stopping you?

ONE SIZE FITS ALL RUNNING SHOES

"As some people who buy these shoes do improve at running, those that fail must lack motivation energy and commitment."

Custom Fit Running Shoes

"Everyone who uses these shoes is successful at significantly improving their performance because these shoes feel comfortable and it's fun to run in them."

A PASSION for the EDGE

LIVING YOUR DREAMS NOW

A PASSION for the EDGE

LIVING YOUR DREAMS NOW

TIM TYLER

EDENSCAPE PUBLISHING

EDENSCAPE PUBLISHING COMPANY
P.O. Box 110650
Anchorage, Alaska 99511-0650

Edenscape Publishing Company books are available at special
quantity discounts for use as premiums, promotions, or text in
company training programs. For more information, please write to
the Director of Special Sales, Edenscape Publishing Company,
P.O. Box 110650, Anchorage, Alaska, 99511-0650.

Edenscape Publishing Company website address:
http://www.edenscapepublishing.com

Printed in the United States of America.

Library of Congress Control Number: 2007909228 (hardcover edition)
Library of Congress Control Number: 2008904569 (softcover edition)

ISBN 978-0-9789786-0-0 (hardcover edition)
ISBN 978-0-9789786-1-7 (softcover edition)
Business-success / Self-help / Autobiography

Designed by Tracy Schwartz

Dedicated to...

...the dreamers of the world, people with thoughts unencumbered by boundaries, those who can look and see the future and wish to move from dreaming to living their dreams. It is possible!

...to my wife Joan, who stands by me in love and gives me the courage to live my dreams. To my children Noel, Shannon, and Cristi, who support me no matter how crazy I get. And to my sister, Jan, who is always there with encouragement for my family and I.

"Everything is possible for him who believes."

MARK 9:23

Contents

PART 1

"Finding The Path"

Preface

Your dream is where you want to be.

"All our dreams can come true – if we have the
courage to pursue them."

WALT DISNEY

"You are never given a 'dream' without also being given
the power to make it come true."

RICHARD BACH

A dream is a visionary creation of the imagination, something notable for its excellence, a strongly desired goal, a
virtuous aspiration. It is a place we would like to be. It is the vital force within our soul, and the water that nourishes our life.

A worthy dream is worthy of living. Many people have a
worthy dream. Many stick their feet into the melodious froth
of a stream, a tributary to the river of their dream, but then
stand until waterlogged, only dreaming. Or they remain forever
bobbing up and down, side-to-side, forward and backward, in
a backwash of good intentions. Few step into the river of their

dream because they are either afraid of the water, or they are not sure how to navigate the currents that will sweep them toward the realization of their dream. If you wish to move from the comfortable shoreline of your dream into the infinitely exciting rush of the river, to live your dream, then this book is for you.

Every day you decide either to live your dream, or to choose an alternate path. And each moment of your life, you are where you are because of the choices you have made. Choosing to live a dream is to choose to have a thrilling experience, one that excites you, that pulls you from your bed each morning, that thrusts you into each new day, and that ignites your passions. Your dreams are attainable, and you can begin living them today. Being able to live your dreams does not depend on whether the economy is up or down, whether you are married or single, or whether you are rich or poor. Living your dreams depends only on the choices you make each day.

Unfortunately, for many people dreams exist merely as mental projections of imaginary places, characterized by fleeting moments of fantasy, and used simply to find brief relief from the mundane reality of their lives. A place yearned for, but never experienced.

You do not have to accept where you are and what you are doing as inevitable. This book will help you discover within yourself the principles and tools that will allow you to transform your dreams from being something imaginary to being something real. It will show you how to begin to live your dreams now. It will lead you to an exhilarating, unexplored world of new perspectives. It will help you to understand that accepting the mundane is neither safer nor easier than living your dreams.

It will give you the power to choose either to continue living an ordinary life, or to plunge into a life churning with anticipation and endless enthusiasm.

The approach, used to show you how to live your dream, is unique. It integrates three powerful learning steps: (1) **understanding** the principles that will allow you to live your dream, (2) **applying** the principles in your daily life, and (3) **showing** what it is like to succeed in living a dream. This learning approach will enable you to apply the principles of success, and immediately make them a part of you. It will make the principles concrete, real, and alive rather than theoretical, abstract, and inanimate.

Tethered to an adventure story about a motorcycle trip through the Alaskan and Canadian wilderness (one of my dreams) are the principles that will allow you to begin living your dreams. The story is extraordinary in that it shows you how to move from dreaming, to living your dreams. It is ordinary in that it is a dream you can see as being possible for anyone to live (important for realizing the full benefit of the three-step approach to learning).

The actions required to start living your dreams are similar to those used to start reading this book. In both cases, only a beginning is necessary to step upon the path, and only a commitment is needed to take the journey. It is the path that defines the journey, and the journey that realizes the destination.

Prologue

Why don't How-To-Succeed books work?
How is this book different?

"When nothing is sure, everything is possible."
MARGARET DRABBLE

"What you do, cannot be separated from what you are."
UNKNOWN

"If you change your beliefs, you will change your results."
BILL WILLIAMS

This is a story of a 6,500-mile motorcycle trip I took during the summer of 1998. It is about a dream lived, a dream that lured me from 60-hour workweeks and hurled me down solitary roads that wandered through Alaska, the Yukon Territories, British Colombia, Alberta, Washington, and Idaho. The journey immersed me in a world of reflective lakes, untamed rivers, entrancing waterfalls, secluded mountain valleys, distant snowcapped peaks, highland meadows filled with seas of wild flowers, and wild animals that regard humans as insignificant aliens in a land they dominate. A world choked with spectacular scenery and poignant, sweet, sticky sensations that nearly suffocated me with intensity and left me gasping for air. A world filled with isolation, childlike awe, and a tantalizing mixture of excitement and fear (like the tingle you feel while careening down an icy slope on a toboggan—it is a breathtaking thrill, pregnant with a sense of being out of control).

By taking this journey, I finally acted on something that for many years I only fantasized about, something I once thought was beyond my grasp. Then I did it, and I reveled in the act of living my dream. It was an exhilarating experience that exceeded my loftiest expectations and it renewed, refreshed, and revitalized my body, mind, and spirit.

Unexpectedly, I found while wrapped in the solitude of this epic motorcycle ride, I had also embarked on a captivating journey of the mind. Awash in the confluence of the physical and mental journeys, my life changed in an exciting and profound way. The trip transformed me from a dreamer, to one who lives my dreams.

During the mental portion of the journey, I came to realize that nothing had prevented me from living this dream earlier. I learned it was not necessary to wait (it never is), and I discovered a model that allows me to begin immediately living any dream I choose to live.

I am motivated in the writing of this book to share this model, to help peel away the barriers preventing you from realizing your full potential, to swing open a door to the idea that anything is possible, and to encourage you to begin living your dreams now. Life is too short to do otherwise.

This book is about how to reach for your dreams, how to

succeed in achieving them, and how to begin your journey today. I chose a story about a motorcycle adventure to illustrate the principles of success because the trip was a dream of mine, and because it catalyzed a dramatic change in my life. The story shows how to apply the success principles in a way that will also allow you to realize your dreams and aspirations. It demonstrates the exciting results that are possible, and it is an example of something challenging yet something I believe everyone can connect with. My hope is that if you taste the fruits of this book, you too will delight in the wondrous flavors of your dreams.

Before the experience of this dualistic journey, I thought there were three sequential steps required to achieve my dreams. These were: (1) to **learn** a new set of skills aligned with my goals—educate myself, (2) to **define and develop success characteristics** that will help me move toward my aspiration—develop new habits, and (3) to **apply my acquired knowledge** and direct it along a path leading toward my dream—start working stepwise toward my dream. On the surface, this approach appeared reasonable. If my dream were to become a racecar driver and to win the Indianapolis 500, I would just need to learn the mechanics and handling characteristics of an automobile, read about and watch what others were doing, improve performance of my car, practice driving it at high speeds, and enter many races. When I became good enough and received enough recognition, I would perhaps, one day, realize my dream of racing in the Indianapolis 500—and if lucky, win the race.

People reaching for success, or reaching for a dream, commonly use this three-step approach. In addition, many writers of success books also tout this general approach, which they break down into five, seven, ten, twelve, or more parts. What makes the approach so sinister is the presence of some truth, blended into a lot of bad practice. The three-step approach can work if your only interest is to do the routine, or if you have no concern with how much time you spend chasing your dreams. However, if you want to achieve the exceptional, to attain what may seem impossible, and do it in record time, then the three-step approach is ineffective at best, and at worst, it is a barrier to success.

When I applied the three-step approach in my life (as elaborated on in the many "how to succeed" books I read), I noticed whenever I assessed my progress, I would repeatedly determine the time would soon be right for pursuing my dream quests. As I analyzed where I was at any given moment, I would find there were still skills I needed to learn, money I needed to save, and experiences I needed to have. I would continually conclude that my plans were developing well, and that it would not be long before I could begin stepping toward my dreams.

However, during the days of solitude and reflection while on my motorcycle trip, I had time to ponder my dream quests, and I recognized that after much time and effort, progress toward realizing my dreams was embarrassingly insignificant. Over the years, the milestones for achieving my dreams continued to drift lifelessly into the future and the hurdles required to fulfill each step along the path got higher. Stunned, I realized that as time passed I had become so comfortable in the quest that motion toward my dreams had all but stopped. The 'to do' list I was working through had lulled me into thinking that making efforts related to my dream quest was the same as making progress. Each step in the process for realizing my dream stealthily replaced the dream, and the process became the focus of my efforts. As a result, I made little progress toward the dream itself even though I was working hard on an ever-increasing number of steps leading toward my dream. I finally understood I had spent years in the quest rather than in the realization of my dreams. This awareness shocked me and helped me to understand the insidious nature of the three-step approach. It is a silent killer of dreams, and of all extraordinary dreams you wish to live.

At that time, I resolved to pull myself out of the spongy bog that mired me down and hampered progress toward the quests of my heart and my passions. As I rode the desolate roads, I began an analysis that eventually defined the principles for achieving your dreams.

I now know there is not a process required before you can begin to live your dreams. There are no first steps. There is just beginning now, at this moment, to live your dream. There are also principles that if you know, and understand, will give you the comfort to start, the knowledge to persist, and a foundation for being successful in living your chosen dreams. Applying these principles allows you to produce astounding results in the business world, it gives Olympic athletes the edge needed to win gold medals, and it lets you accomplish seemingly impossible feats. Applying these principles will help you to succeed in realizing your dreams.

The principles in this book, while I knew them earlier (individually and theoretically), coalesced and came alive during my motorcycle trip. The dewy condensation of their power covered me, and the world in which I lived, and transformed the way I am.

I moved from planning to live my dreams, to living my dreams.

One of the dreams I had, which persisted for two decades, was to step outside corporate America. I did exactly that shortly after this motorcycle trip. My motivation was to spend more time with my wife and children, to help improve the quality of life for people within our community, to travel, and to earn a living doing what I passionately enjoy—writing, investing, and starting and running my own business. These are all things I am currently doing; these are all things, which in the dimly lit past before my transformation, I only dreamed of doing.

The story in this book will help you learn how to live your dreams now, and to understand, apply, and own the principles of success. It will take you from knowing the words to understanding the meaning.

While reading this book, you will learn the principles of success through self-discovery, and by applying these principles in your everyday life, you will make them yours in a new and powerful way. Making the principles a part of the way you live will enable you to walk successfully through the rest of your life. These principles apply to anything you wish to succeed in, they never change, they will work in every endeavor, and they will help you to succeed in any passion you have, in any area you choose: business, sports, hobbies, public speaking, family, marriage, politics, academics, religion, science, traveling. You complete the list. What do you want most from your life? What dreams do you have?

However, before beginning, there is background information required to lay the foundation for the principles of success illustrated in this story.

* * * * *

Have you ever asked, "Why do people succeed," "Is the ability to succeed a talent everyone has or is it a gift enjoyed only by a favored few," or "Is it possible to succeed in anything I set my mind to?" I wanted to know the answers to these questions, so I started reading about successful people and began testing, in my own life, the theories in books that contained many of the fashionable and best-known success ideas of the day.

In reading biographies of successful people, I found there is not a one-to-one relationship between success and intelligence, or good looks, or charisma, or being born into money, or many other characteristics widely believed necessary to be successful in life. Also, in studying people that have been successful in business, sports, academics, politics, and movies, I found many came from a station in life similar to my own and have overcome obstacles as great as, or even much greater than, the obstacles I face in my personal quest for success.

I have personally known geniuses. They were gifted people who breezed through college and could do anything they set their mind to. One of them is now a clerk in a chain store. It is not my intention to belittle the position of a clerk. I was a clerk in a chain store and thoroughly enjoyed this job. Any honest work is honorable. The point here is that there was a stark contrast between my expectations of what this person might be doing and what he is doing. I have also known people who barely made it through high school, but became multimillionaires in the time it took me to go through college and start working in my first job. Again, my expectations were shattered. I am sure you have made similar observations in either your personal lives or in the public lives of people you admire.

On the surface, these observations did not make sense and I searched to understand why some people succeed despite facing great obstacles, while others fail even though they have all the intellect, money, and talents that should have guaranteed success. I had dreams of a life that stretched the limits of what I believed was possible, and I wanted to find the tools that would allow me to realize my aspirations. Even though I read books on how to be successful, and even though I applied the ideas in these books, I found they had little or no lasting influence on me. What made these books so ineffective in changing my life?

There seems to be three key problems in many of the how-to-succeed books that stifled life-changing transformations. These are the problems with lists, living the lists, and language.

So, what's so bad about lists?

Many books written on the topic of how to succeed typically summarize themselves with a **list**. The list contains anywhere from five, to seven, to twelve, to over a hundred items. Each item on the list is an action, characteristic, principle, or concept. These books also present compelling arguments for why we must do each item on the list to become successful. However, lists are not helpful because items on a list do not readily translate to your specific situation, or items on the list may not directly affect what you are trying to accomplish and thus become a distraction, or the list does not include a critical action needed to ensure your success. As a result, lists fail to make a lasting impact on your daily actions and they do not result in a significant beneficial change in your life.

In addition, some lists contain elements about how to change you—how to make you "better." What's implied is that you must change in some way to be successful. These changes include such actions as mastering the art of communication, getting to know important and influential people, becoming better educated, improving your vocabulary, or changing your personality. There is nothing wrong with any of these activities. However, it is misleading and distracting to suggest they are preconditions to success. There are many examples of successful people who were not great communicators, who did not get to know important or influential people (however, once they were successful many important and influential people got to know them), who were uneducated, who did not have an impressive vocabulary, and who had the same personality they were born with. The secret of success is not about changing what you are; instead, it is about being true to who you are. It is about what you believe. It is about knowing who you are and leveraging your essence in a way that enables you to realize your full potential. It is about finding the source of power within you, harnessing it, and directing it to achieve your dreams.

Another problem with lists is that many people believe that if just given the answer, the list, the ideas, they will possess the knowledge and have the power to evoke the "magic" imparted by the words. This belief is deceptive and destructive. The hope of an instant, no-bother, and no-effort cure is symptomatic of a fundamental problem we must purge from our lives to be successful.

Let us consider this point for a moment. One of my hobbies is numismatics. To be an expert in this field you must be able to:

- Effectively grade coins
- Identify varieties and errors
- Detect counterfeits
- Understand toning
- Effectively preserve coins
- Learn the manufacturing processes
- Be knowledgeable about commemoratives
- Provide quick and accurate valuations
- Build a quality collection

You have the list, so now you too are a numismatist. Of course, this is a ridiculous statement.

However, I know many intelligent people who fall into the trap of thinking that they just need a list to become proficient in an area such as "how to succeed." That is because carefully crafted one-liners appear to them to represent the essence of success ("Build relationships with the right people," "Commit to your vision," "Be proactive," "Strive for excellence," "Build self-esteem," "Get organized"). It is easy to fall into the trap of believing that by putting a list on the wall, you can immediately begin to access the knowledge embedded within the words, and become successful.

I once attended an organizational learning course where the instructors refused to provide a summary list of course principles until the end of the week. It drove many of the participants crazy. The "listoholics" just wanted the answers so they could get on with applying the principles from the course. It seemed to them a waste of time to spend several hours a day just talking about the value of using simple models for organizational learning, how actions influence responses, and how individual learning differs from team learning. They just wanted the list of principles, and did not wish to bother with the details.

This book differs from other books on success in that it does not promote the use of lists. Instead, the intent is to create a literary work that will allow you to discover the key elements of success as they apply specifically, and uniquely, to you and your situation. I believe that if you are told the secrets of success you will forget (or they will have no lasting impact on your life). However, if you discover the secrets of success that apply specifically to you, they will be remembered, and if you practice the secrets of success, you will master the art of succeeding. This work creates an opportunity for discovering and applying the principles that will allow you to succeed in living your dreams. By the end of this book, you will be able to define the principles that are specific to your situation, your aspiration, and your dream. You will have tools necessary to begin the journey. Then, all you will need to do is take the step. Live your dream.

O.K., so a list hanging on a wall isn't going to change my life, but what's wrong with giving actions for living the list?

Naturally, books written on how to succeed provide more than just a list. They generally spend several chapters on each item on the list and show how some successful people have incorporated a listed item into their daily lives. A problem here is in "the giving" of the lists or principles, because what is given and the way it is illustrated may not readily translate to your situation or relate to the specific activity in which you wish to succeed.

For example, if I were to write a book on how to live a long and healthy life, one of the principles in a list might be to "be safe." There is no question this is an important principle for living a long and healthy life, and it is easy to accept this principle without question or further thought. The killer here is the belief that you have found an answer to living a long and healthy life in the words "be safe." What does "be safe" mean to you personally? The list of things that must be considered to "be safe" is endless—going down the stairs, crossing the street, cutting an apple, climbing a ladder, mowing a lawn, driving a car, riding a bike, hiking in the mountains, and on, and on, and on, and on, and on. It becomes overwhelming because it is too broad an idea to be useful. The concept "be safe" covers the entire world and all we do in it. In addition, it is not meaningful to you because it is not personalized. It does not connect to you and your specific situation. Because of these problems, "be safe" will not ignite a flame within you. It will have an "of course," "naturally" or "so what" flavor about it, and so it will not influence your day-to-day actions.

On the other hand, if I wrote a book that allowed you to **discover** (without saying the words) that one of the key principles behind a long and healthy life is being safe, in your discovery of the principle you would **translate** it in a way that was useful and personally meaningful to you. A truck driver or a traveling salesman might translate the discovered principle to "drive safely." A commuter in New York City might translate it to "be aware of your surroundings." An industrial worker might translate it to "wear your personal protective equipment" (steel-toed shoes, gloves, safety glasses, and hardhat). These translations are much more effective than "be safe" because they both personalize the idea and move it from an idea to a specific action you can do each day—"drive safely," "be aware of your surroundings," and "wear your personal protective equipment."

In addition, translating the concept "be safe" to a specific action, associated with something that is a large part of your life, will result in the concept spilling over into the rest of your life by way of consistent actions. The habit of safe actions in one area leads to safe actions in other areas of your life. If you always wear your seat belt at work, you will likely also wear your seat belt when not working. It will become a way of life. A passion. This illustrates why it is essential for you to discover the principles of success, rather than just given a list or a set of actions. In your discovery of the principles, you will translate each principle into a form that is useful, meaningful, and powerful to you. By putting the principle into an action that relates to succeeding in your specific aspiration, it will become a part of you, and will immediately begin to move you toward your dream.

Therefore, the discovery of concepts, and the translation of concepts into actions expressed in your own words and relevant to your own situation, is a critical process. It makes the principles specific, personal, and meaningful to you. It transforms the concept from merely an idea to something you can do—an action. And action is the only way to get results.

Finally, how can language affect your ability to succeed?

In addition to the importance of discovery and translation of the principles that will allow you to be successful, it is critical to understand the impact **language** can have on our view of the world, how it both creates and reinforces our daily reality, and how it affects our understanding of, or belief in, what is possible. The only way we know the world in which we live is through our language. Therefore, language can be a strength or a weakness. It has the power to either propel us upward to unimaginable heights or confine us to the darkest depths of our past experiences and current perceptions.

Our view of the world, based on language, has obvious pitfalls we need to avoid. We can be deceived by statements that are extrapolated from experiences; or by statements made as fact, that are accepted as truth and go unchallenged. (Deception by language is an abstract and difficult concept in which an entire book could be written and it is a concept that will be examined several times in the story following this prologue).

It is through language we gather general facts and develop interpretations based on our experiences and the experiences of others. Our conditioning makes us believe that the views we have are true. We then use every bit of evidence aligned with our views as an opportunity to reinforce and strengthen them. We believe we live in an objective world where everything is real and has substance. However, what we call a fact might not be a fact, because information or facts we extract from one experience may not be relevant when applied to a different situation, or from a different perspective.

For example, if I lived in a city and drove to the country, I might describe a narrow, poorly maintained, two-lane asphalt road as rough and dangerous. However, if I lived on a large remote farm, surrounded by dirt and gravel roads, I might describe the same narrow, poorly maintained, two-lane asphalt road as smooth and safe. Both descriptions are factual and truthful from each person's perspective. And both people, when relating the condition of this road to a third party not familiar with the area, would paint different pictures of what the road was like.

Therefore, our knowledge of any situation, where information about that situation is extracted from external sources or extrapolated from others experience, could be either appropriate or inappropriate for our purpose, correct or incorrect, true or false. The information may either help us or be a barrier to our success. Disturbing? Yes, because if we are moving toward a dream and we believe something is true that is actually false or does not apply in our case, this misleading information may create an imaginary obstacle to our success.

We must intimately know the truth for any given situation and not be intellectually deceived by inappropriate extrapolation of information we have gathered, or by others' perceptions of what truth is from their point of view. Facts do not interpret themselves—people interpret facts. Everyone's preferences, views, needs, desires, and life directions are different. Therefore, our translation of a fact to a concept, or the translation of other people's "truths" to a concept that applies to us, are subject to error when applied to a specific situation—when applied to living our dream. The best way to know the truth is by doing.

Deceptions by language can also occur from statements that appear factual and are therefore accepted at face value. For example, if a person says, "I could never become a millionaire," the very act of stating it makes it true for them. The way this person talks, the way he acts, how he is motivated, and the way he responds to every situation in his life will reinforce the position "I could never become a millionaire." In making the statement, it becomes a "fact," and the person's subconscious will work overtime to find evidence to reinforce this "fact."

This person, when asked why he cannot become a millionaire, will say there are many obstacles preventing him from acquiring a million dollars. However, those obstacles exist only because he or others say they exist, and for no other reason. The obstacles are only in the mind. In reality, obstacles to living your dreams do not exist. There is nothing concrete out there that we can touch, or even define, that is an obstacle to success. This point is so important that it is worth stating it again. An obstacle is merely a creation of our mind and does not exist in fact. An obstacle to our success is not real and does not exist.

Let us examine typical obstacles people create to convince themselves that they cannot become a millionaire, and then try to discover if the specific obstacle believed to be preventing them from achieving this goal is real or imaginary. We can do this using the following make-believe dialogue between two people.

"I could never become a millionaire because it takes money to make money and I don't have any money."

"So what is the obstacle preventing you from getting the money you need?"

"My job pays only enough to get by on. I'm living from one paycheck to the next."

"So what is the obstacle preventing you from making more money?"

"I don't have the skills I need to get a higher paying job."

"So what's the obstacle preventing you from getting the skills for a higher paying job?"

"I don't have the money I need for school, so I can learn the skills needed to do what I would like to do—I'm barely getting by now."

"So what is the obstacle preventing you from getting the money for school?"

"Well, I cannot save any money on my current salary."

"So what's the obstacle preventing you from getting an educational loan?"

This sort of conversation could go on indefinitely and it could go down many paths. In fact, when you probe for the perceived obstacles (lack of money, lack of skills, lack of education), you find there is nothing tangible that stops you from taking the next step—if you want to. Facing an obstacle, trying to define it, and searching for a tangible aspect to it is the best way to make the obstacle vanish.

"I could never become a millionaire," is an example of a view formed through a collection of interpretations from various situations in your life. This "fact" is then reinforced with obstacles believed to be real, but on examination, the obstacles do not exist.

This exercise helps to demonstrate the important role language can play in reaching for and achieving your dreams, and helps to illustrate there is no such thing as obstacles preventing you from doing what you sincerely wish to do. Obstacles are merely reasons we use to justify our inaction and to excuse failure.

The magic here is knowing that when you look for the imagined obstacle and when you reach out and try to touch it, the obstacle vanishes. It exists only because you say it exists. It is not there. Try probing for an obstacle in your life that is preventing you from reaching an important goal or dream, and see if you can make it materialize. Are you surprised? Did you find a solution or solutions to move past the "obstacle?" Where there is a solution, there is no "obstacle." Obstacles to success, to living your dream, do not exist. Period. There is always a path that will take you forward.

One obstacle our imaginary protagonist was stumbling over is a common excuse for not succeeding—money. Many examples could be used to demonstrate the belief that "it takes money to make money," is false; however, there is one that I believe vividly makes the point.

Tom First and Tom Scott started up Nantucket Nectars during the winter of 1989/90 with only $100.00. In 1999, Nantucket Nectars employed over 100 people, distributed its products in over 30 states and 5 countries, and was worth millions of dollars. There is nothing new about bottled fruit juice. Tom and Tom made their product distinct by keeping high standards, staying focused on their values, believing passionately in what they were doing, and persisting with their vision. They remained in action and did not waver from their goals. It only took $100.00 to start down the road to millions. Money was not an obstacle.

The reverse of the "I could never become a millionaire," example is also true. If a person says, "I will become a millionaire," and believes it, the act of stating it makes it true to them. The way this person talks, the way he acts, and the way he responds to situations will reinforce the position "I will become a millionaire." This statement can be even more powerful by naming a specific month and year in which they will become a millionaire and by visualizing the path, or steps, to get there. The more specific the statement is, the more clearly defined the path, the more powerful it is in allowing you to realize your goal.

For me, John F. Kennedy dramatically makes this point in his speech at Rice University on September 12, 1962.

"We choose to go to the moon. We choose to go to the moon in this decade and do the other things, not because they are easy, but because they are hard, because that goal will serve to organize and measure the best of our energies and skills, because that challenge is one that we are willing to accept, one we are unwilling to postpone, and one which we intend to win.

"The growth of our science and education will be enriched by new knowledge of our universe and environment, by new techniques of learning of our universe and environment, by new techniques of learning and mapping and observation, by new tools and computers for industry, medicine, the home as well as the school.

"But if I were to say, my fellow citizens, that we shall send to the moon, 240,000 miles away from the control station in Houston, a giant rocket more than three hundred feet tall, the length of this football field, made of new metal alloys, some of which have not yet been invented, capable of standing heat and stresses several times more than ever been experienced, fitted together with a precision better than the finest watch, carrying all the equipment needed for propulsion, guidance, control, communications, food and survival, on an untried mission, to an unknown celestial body, and then return it safely to earth, re-entering the atmosphere at speeds of over 25,000 miles per hour, causing heat about half of the temperature of the sun ..... and do all this, and do it

*right, and do it first before this decade is out—then we
must be bold."*

Notice the great clarity in which John F. Kennedy described
his dream. It is the clarity, the feeling that you can actually see
us doing this great thing, which propelled the nation forward.
President Kennedy captured the imagination of the world when
he spoke these words. In this speech, he outlined the goal of
sending a man to the moon within ten years, how we would accomplish this challenge, and the benefits we would enjoy when
we succeeded. The simplicity and lucidity of his vision caused
his every action to reinforce the realization of this dream, which
resulted in success (even though many eminent scientists of the
day thought it would require closer to a century to meet the
challenge). His vision was powerful. Fourteen months and ten
days after giving this speech at Rice University, John F. Kennedy
died from an assassin's bullet, but his dream lived on and we are
still seeing the benefits from his vision.

Another striking feature of President Kennedy's speech was
the daring stand taken when he said, "We choose to go to the
moon in this decade ... because (it is) hard; because that goal
will serve to organize and measure the best of our energies and
skills ... ." He did not say, "Let us try." He said, "We choose to
go to the moon this decade ... ." He defined a goal that appeared
to be possible but just beyond our reach to, " ... serve to organize
and measure the best of our energies and skills ... ." He did this
to challenge us in a way that would bring out the best in us as in-
dividuals and as a nation. This must have been a great political
risk, but to succeed in producing spectacular results you must
be willing to take risks. Greatness does not grow from medioc-

rity; it grows out of the exceptional.

As mentioned previously, in this book I will use the method of discovery and translation to show you how to live your dream now by helping you uncover the specific principles for success that apply to you and your dream. These principles will let you start and persist down the path of living your chosen dreams. Therefore, to maximize the benefit derived from this book, you should take a moment now to write down something you would specifically like to be successful at, a dream you would like to begin living now, and keep this goal in mind as you read the book. Visualize your dream. Picture the benefits from achieving your dream. Be as specific as possible. Define the date by which you will achieve your dream. Stretch yourself by making the goal one you cannot at this time see how to accomplish. Make it a goal or dream that you are passionate about achieving, one that is challenging, that stretches you, and that is worthy of your time and efforts. See if you can define your dream as vividly as John F. Kennedy defined his dream for sending a man to the moon.

Writing your goal is many times more powerful than just thinking about it, because writing it makes the goal concrete, writing it helps you express the goal with clarity, writing it makes the goal specific, and the written goal becomes a contract you have with yourself.

If you want to make your dream a reality, take the time now to write your specific goal, with clarity, on the page provided at the back this book so you can review it as you are reading. Select a dream you are passionate about living. Also, write down the key principles, actions, and ideas you discover that apply specifically to you and to your dream.

While reading this book, take time to understand the success principles (discovery). Write them down within the context of an action toward your goal (translation). Think about the principles as you read, become comfortable with them, mold them into your style, and start applying them. This will actively translate your learnings to your specific goal or dream, provide a foundation for stepping forward, and help you to break through apparent barriers with confidence. The success principles you discover and formulate for your aspiration, combined with taking the position that barriers to achieving your goals do not exist, will allow you to move down the road of success, to maintain momentum, and to propel you toward your dream. If you do these things, you can realize your personal dreams.

Finally, I have no intention to give advice. Instead, I will provide you with the principles that you can apply to any personal challenge, any goal, or any dream you wish to achieve. These principles work. Take the time to make them a part of you. By applying the principles you will own them. You will then be able to use them on any other goal or dream you might have, and by making them a part of the way you live, they will enrich you for the rest of your life.

This book will get you started down the road to success; however, the journey can only be yours to take. The approach in this book will allow you to interpret the success principles in a way that relates to you and the specific area in which you wish to be successful.

The example used to illustrate these principles is not one of a corporate CEO that miraculously turns a dying company around and makes it a brilliant success—although the principles will allow you that kind of success. In contrast, this story is about something I hope each of you can relate to, and can see as possible in your own life. It is about taking a three-week motorcycle trip through a rugged and pristine country. It is about your discovery of the success principles that can help you to master any challenge, or to realize any dream you have. At the same time, it is about the rich and unexpected rewards derived from living your dreams.

Enjoy the journeys—the motorcycle trip and the discovery of principles that will help you to succeed in living your dreams.

PART 2

"Starting the Journey"

An Invitation To Start Living Your Dream

"Security is mostly a superstition. It does not exist in nature, nor do the children of men as a whole experience it. Avoiding danger is no safer in the long run than outright exposure. Life is either a daring adventure or nothing."
HELEN KELLER

"There is no security on this earth; there is only opportunity."
DOUGLAS MACARTHUR

I promise you freedom, the wind, and success—nothing more. I invite you to journey with me if you are a seeker, someone who must know, one with an intensity to be in action, a player in life. However, if you come, prepare yourself to leave this journey forever changed, expanded beyond the elastic limits of your current existence, incapable of contracting back into the world from whence you came.

I make the promise, I define the peril, choose now to come with me on this journey, or stay behind. In life, there are no fences to sit on.

Passion Has Power

"By believing passionately in something
that still does not exist, we create it. The non-existent
is whatever we have not sufficiently desired."

NICOS KAZANTSAKIS

"Passion is Powerful ... nothing was ever achieved without it,
and nothing can take its place. No matter what you face in life,
if your passion is great enough, you will find the strength to succeed.
Without passion, life has no meaning. So put your heart, mind,
and soul into even your smallest acts ... this is the essence of passion.
This is the secret to life."

UNKNOWN

"If you don't take risks, you don't gain anything."

BRIDGET FONDA

I am not exactly sure when the fire began to rage. I only faintly remember a glowing ember, nestled in the woods, blown by a gentle breeze. At first, the ember glowed a pale red. As time passed, the glow brightened, and turned a blinding white. Then a wisp of smoke appeared. An occasional flame struck out against the breeze, but the gentle wind that nurtured life also extinguished it. Life flickered tenuously between extermination and existence. Finally, a flame exploded from within the tinder that held it captive, and the fire became unquenchable. The wind no longer subdued the flames—it intensified the heat and flames erupted consuming all they touched.

This is what happened to me. My passion was the ember, motorcycles were the breezes, and life was the nested tender waiting to feed an unquenchable flame of passion.

* * * * *

I grew up in Walla Walla, a small southeastern Washington town surrounded by endless fields of wheat and situated at the base of the Blue Mountains. One hot Midsummer Day when I was fourteen, for no reason that I can recall, my father brought home a Yamaha 55 motor scooter. The spontaneity of this act had all the excitement of Christmas attached to it, with none of the agonizing anticipation. At that time, I had a brother and five sisters (my sixth sister was a joy and a surprise who showed up a couple of years later). When my father rode up to the house on the motor scooter, a horde of children descended on him (half family, half neighborhood kids), and everyone delighted in a ride on the scooter around the field behind our house. After several weeks, my dad started to let me ride solo and then, probably out of exhaustion rather than complete confidence in my skills, he started letting me give my brother and sisters rides around the field. While the enthusiasm of the rest of the family faded with time, the scooter captivated me and I spent many long summer days riding in the gravel pits near our home and exploring country roads (in a small farming town like Walla Walla, a driver's license was not required for kids to drive on the streets, it just made it legal).

Later my father negotiated the purchase of a Suzuki dealership and he started bringing home bigger and faster motorcycles to try out. I enjoyed riding, but at this time in my life, riding was just a seed, the ember barely glowed. Before long, I was sixteen and cars, pretty girls, and the distractions of the sixties began to block the breeze that fanned the ember within my soul.

The next experience with motorcycles was three years later. I was in the military and worked in the Minuteman missile R&D program at Vandenberg Air Force Base, California. This was a high activity period during the development of the multiple warhead deployment system on the Minuteman, and for a time we were launching two to three missiles a week. I was an electronics specialist responsible for maintaining the ground station, the launch control center, and the telemetry package on the missile itself. My wife, Joni, and I lived on base, in a trailer court. We were young; we were in love; we were in California; and I launched missiles for a living. Life was good.

Some friends of ours, Roy and Phyllis Siedohff, lived in a trailer near us and they both had motorcycles. Even though most of my riding up to that point had been off the road, I had never ridden a motorcycle specifically designed for off-road use, and I was not prepared for the experience I was about to have. The Siedohff's had two Kawasaki 125 motocross motorcycles. Roy took me out to ride in some gravel pits on the military base. The rat-a-tat-tat beat of the engine reverberating in my chest evoked a primitive spirit within, and the throttle unleashed torque I had never before experienced. A twist of the wrist produced compliance from the motorcycle by lifting the front wheel off the ground and trying to shove it down my throat. When we were not launching missiles, Roy and I repaired, talked about, or rode motorcycles every chance we had. The ember again glowed for a brief time, and then when I was discharged from the service it cooled.

After serving in the military, my wife Joni, our new daughter Noel, and I moved to Washington State where I studied chemical engineering at Washington State University. From this point life blurred past, marked by a university degree, two more wonderful children (Shannon and Cristi), and several white-collar jobs in California, Texas, North Dakota, England, and Alaska.

Then, twenty-seven years after my last ride on a motorcycle, while living in Anchorage, Alaska, something started fanning the ember again. I do not know where it came from or why the breeze began to stir, I only know that the long dormant ember once again started to glow. Ever so slightly, the temperature began to rise. Occasionally, I talked about getting a motorcycle. My wife, Joni, threw cold water at the idea, but she never threw it directly on the nearly imperceptible and fragile ember, so the glow continued to grow. When I saw a motorcycle, I would make a comment about it; when I bought a pair of boots needed for work I referred to them as my motorcycle boots; and when I talked with family and friends, we exchanged fanciful stories about motorcycles. The passion grew and wove itself almost imperceptibly into my life.

Passion is like magic; it is incredible. When you have passion, when it burns in your soul, it pulls power from the entire universe, and it enables you to accomplish anything.

One day I was driving home past a Honda dealership and saw a Shadow motorcycle strategically placed next to the front showroom window. The classic lines caught my eye. I stopped and went in—just to look.

Inside the shop were dirt bikes, sports bikes, custom bikes, and touring bikes. It was the custom bikes that initially caught my eye: the Magna, the Shadow A.L.E., and the Shadow Spirit. I was looking these over and discussing details about each one with the salesperson. Then I wandered past a Valkyrie and the spark that had been contained and hidden within me instantly ignited and I knew the flames could not be subdued. I looked at the Valkyrie; I walked around it; I sat on it; I started it; I listened to it; I had to have it.

When I went home that evening I was reserved and calm, but what I had seen kept rolling and churning inside my head, kept glowing and burning within my soul. During dinner that night, I casually mentioned to Joni that I had seen the motor-cycle of my dreams.

"What kind was it?" Joni asked.

"A Valkyrie, made by Honda." I said.

"Is it the best?"

"Yes, for what I wanted to do, mainly riding around the countryside and touring. It's absolutely the best."

"There isn't one that is better?" she queried one more time.

"No."

"Then get it."

"Then get it," she said as casually as "pass the salad" or "would you like some more potatoes?" Then get it! The words exploded in my ears and electricity danced inside my head. My wife is empathetic. She has a deep sense of what others need and responds unselfishly to these needs, an endearing quality of hers. However, I never expected this reply.

Passion is magic. It is contagious. It is infectious. It feeds the burning ember, and strengthens the breeze that keeps the fire burning inside.

"No, I shouldn't." I said.

"Why not?"

"It's too much money."

"You've worked hard for the money we have. If you want the motorcycle, buy it."

I do not recall much that happened after that, I just remember the words "buy it" endlessly echoing inside my head.

I went back down to the store a few days later—just to look. The Valkyrie I saw earlier was still there. Red and white with leather seats, leather saddlebags, and chrome everywhere. After a few minutes, Katie, the sales representative who had helped me earlier in the week, came over.

"How much for the Valkyrie?" I asked—still just looking.

"$15,999."

Then, without realizing how it happened, "just looking" turned into "I'M BUYING."

"I'll give you $15,000 for it," I said while trying to conceal my enthusiasm and hide the drool oozing from the corners of my mouth. Enthusiasm and drool are both clear indications to any seasoned sales representative that I would instantly accept a counteroffer that was higher than the tag price.

"I'll have to take your offer to the manager," Katie said, and she walked over to an office in the corner of the showroom.

I stood there nonchalantly drooling and continued to casually look the Valkyrie over. I hoped my offer was acceptable because I did not know how long I could maintain my calm, cool demeanor. When Katie came out of the office and started my way, I pretended not to see her and just kept looking at the Valkyrie—drooling.

"Your offer was approved by Tony, our sales manager," Katie said.

"Great!" I said as a smile began to grow across my face. "I'll arrange for a loan at my bank and we can close on Saturday." In the half dreaming, half drooling, semiconscious state I was in, I totally forgot Saturday was my wife's birthday.

On Saturday morning, Joni understood, but I could tell by her subtle facial expressions, the tone of her voice, and the heavy static ladened air that rippled around her; I could tell as though clairvoyance was thrust upon me this day and all her thoughts were loudly spoken in my mind; I could tell that her understanding was draining, slowly, like the sap in leaves touched by the icy chill of an early fall morning.

"It will only take a couple of hours to close." I said, "I will be home before lunch and we will spend the rest of the day together." A somewhat strained but cordial smile gave all the reply that was necessary.

Joni and I arrived downtown at the dealership, Honda of Anchorage, just as it opened its doors for the day. Joni dropped me off and I went inside. Katie had all the paperwork put together. I sat down at the desk, we chatted for a few minutes, and then we began going through the process of exchanging a promise to pay for the keys to the Valkyrie. This was a simple process in concept. I signed the loan papers, we filled out the application for title and registration, and mounted the temporary plate on the motorcycle. Then the unexpected happened. Out of the desk drawer came endless checklists we had to go over and sign:

salesperson quality check, salesperson administration check, customer information check, motorcycle set-up and predelivery check, and customer vehicle familiarization.

I could see how this was all very useful to someone like me, who had not owned a motorcycle in a long time. I could also see how sitting around talking about motorcycles could be enjoyable. However, today was my wife's birthday, I was out buying myself a motorcycle, and I sensed a strange chill in the warm summer air as minutes grew to hours. By early afternoon, we finally finished all the required paperwork. Katie put copies of everything inside an envelope, handed me the keys, and we went outside behind the shop where the Valkyrie was all prepped and waiting. Here I received a few final instructions like the pattern for shifting the gears, how to turn on the gas, the location of the front wheel lock, and the function of the various buttons. I am glad we did this because I would feel real dumb going back inside complaining about the motorcycle not starting only to find out the gas valve had not been turned on.

There was an 'L' shaped parking lot along the back and one side of the store, and there were no cars parked in it at this time. I asked if it would be all right if I rode the Valkyrie around the parking lot for a while to get the feel of it before I headed home.

"No problem, take your time and enjoy your new motorcycle," Katie said.

Thankfully, she went back inside and left me alone to relearn the basics of riding a motorcycle. Like a child walking for the first time in shoes, I knew the mechanics of riding a motorcycle but the application felt foreign and unnatural. It had been 27 years since I had even been on a motorcycle, I had never ridden anything larger then a 250 cc motorcycle, and I had just climbed onto the most powerful factory-made, custom motorcycle in the world. The Valkyrie weighs over 700 pounds, has a silky smooth shaft drive, a five-speed constant-mesh transmission, and a 1520 cc, in-line 6 cylinder engine, tricked up with six carburetors, and six exhaust pipes all working together to deliver 105 barely tamed horses of power, and neatly placed in a classic cruiser frame. I began to wonder if I had gone insane without noticing.

The motorcycle bug had bitten my younger brother Lloyd a few years earlier, but he sensibly took things in stages. He started back into motorcycling by buying himself and his wife, Jenny, a Honda Nighthawk 250 cc motorcycle. A year or so later they both upgraded. Jenny got a Yamaha Virago 535 cc and Lloyd got a Honda Magna 750 cc motorcycle. Jenny still had her Virago when Lloyd upgraded one more time to Honda ST1100 V-4 sport touring motorcycle with more speed and power.

In contrast, I decided to just go straight to the endpoint—the motorcycle of my dreams. Even though I knew it was logical to take things in stages (the sane approach), and even though I knew that this was much more bike then I could handle, I also knew that it was possible for me to expertly ride the Valkyrie. After all, I had ridden motorcycles before. I would just have to work the wrinkles out as I went along. Besides, the Valkyrie was mine now and there was no turning back. I was on the beach of an unexplored island and had burned all the ships needed for a safe retreat. My only choice now was to explore the island and learn how to survive on it.

I sat on my shiny new Valkyrie, set the gas valve to on, turned the key, opened the choke, shifted into neutral, and hit the start button. A spark ignited within the engine and the motorcycle responded with a deep throaty rumble that was more like an Indy 500 racecar than a motorcycle. At that moment a million questions exploded in my mind, "What am I doing?" "Can I ride this thing?" "Am I crazy?" With the rumble of the engine resonating inside my chest, I put on my helmet, pulled on my leather gloves, and sat for a minute to let the engine warm up, and to soak in the statically charged reality of the moment. Then I turned the choke off and gave the throttle a few quick twists. The thunder reverberated within my chest causing my heart to race along with the engine. The excitement was building—clutch in, shift to first gear, and a very slow release of the clutch. I was careful because I did not know how far I had to release the hand clutch to find the friction point, and there was no way I wanted to engage the clutch too quickly because I knew the motorcycle could easily leave without me.

When my left hand was halfway open, the Valkyrie started to roll forward. I kept the clutch at the friction point because I was heading from the heel to the end of the short leg of the 'L' shaped parking area and needed to start a right-handed turn. The motorcycles I had ridden previously were all relatively small and when you wanted to maneuver them, you could just horse them around.

It was at the first turn I learned lesson number one: you do not horse a Valkyrie around. You learn what the Valkyrie likes to do, how it likes to move, and you conform to the motorcycle.

O.K. I got around the corner, not smoothly, but I did negotiate the turn. The second turn at the end of the short leg of the 'L' came too quickly so I pulled the clutch in, stopped, and from a seated position pushed the motorcycle back far enough to make another run at the corner. I was feeling very awkward. Now off I went back toward the heel of the 'L' and down the long side of the parking lot. I rode as far as possible on the left side of the lot, slowed, and turned at a modest pace letting the boot on my right foot drag along the asphalt.

Not too bad. I went through the 'L' pattern again and could already feel myself improving. The third time around I shifted from first to second gear as I raced down the long side of the lot. On the fourth time around, as I started the right hand "U" turn at the end of the long section of the parking lot, it was apparent I was going too fast and would hit the wall of the motorcycle shop if I did not slow down. Since my brake foot was dragging on the asphalt surface, I lightly touched the hand brake.

Instantly, I learned lesson number two: do not use only the front brake while turning a corner, particularly with gravel on the surface. Before I knew what happened, my brand-new Valkyrie was lying on its right side in the parking lot and I was standing next to it, staring.

Surprisingly, my first thought was, "wow, what a marvelous piece of engineering." In assessing the damage, I found the handlebars, saddlebags, muffler, turn signals, rearview mirror, and all the chrome had escaped the crash without any damage. There were just three points touching the ground—the two tires and one point on the engine case guard. Not a scratch anywhere except for a minor scrape on the case guard.

My second thought was of a telephone conversation I had some months earlier with my brother Lloyd. He had mentioned a list of motorcycling rules he developed and referred to as the motorcyclists' bible. One of his rules, "don't buy a motorcycle you cannot lift," was ricocheting around inside my head. Would I have to go back inside the shop only minutes after buying the Valkyrie and ask someone to help me pick it up? Dread of dreads.

I thought the bike would be much too heavy to just pick up, so I pushed it forward as I lifted with the idea to roll it up. The 700+ pounds did not budge. The thought of asking someone for help encouraged me to try one more time, or to try forever if that was how long it would take to get the motorcycle upright. Even though I did not think it would work, on the next try I decided to just pick the bike straight up. Success! The center of gravity on the Valkyrie was so low I only had to lift about 150 pounds to tilt it back to vertical.

Having the Valkyrie upright I threw my leg over the seat, sat down, pushed the start button, and nonchalantly looked around to see if anyone had witnessed what must have been a comical sight. No one was around except a couple of mechanics in a service bay at the other end of the lot, and they either did not see what had just happened or politely ignored the episode. I preferred to assume they had not seen anything so I could keep my self-esteem intact.

I now started to get philosophical. Everyone lays his motorcycle down at least once. Now that I had dumped mine, there was one less thing I had to worry about.

After a couple more times around the parking lot, I decided I was ready to ride on the street. The trip home went across town, onto a freeway, and through the suburbs to our house. I still had not mastered the synchronization of clutch, gears, and awesome power, but I was sure no one noticed the jerky transitions between gears and the screaming engine sounds as I went from one traffic light to the next (I was still trying to keep my ego intact). Finally, after a dozen traffic lights of embarrassment, I was on the highway and cruising at 55 mph.

The next thing I needed to concentrate on was practicing so I could become proficient enough to pass the motorcycle-riding test, obtain my license, and legally ride on the street. However, once home I quickly realized the next thing I really needed to concentrate on was my wife's birthday—whoops.

Even though I did get home a little late, my wife had the wonderful birthday she deserved. We had a family get-together, followed by presents, and then dinner at one of Joni's favorite restaurants—The Corsair. The Corsair is a French restaurant with spectacular food, an exquisite wine list, and a romantic atmosphere. We all enjoyed being together and finished off a perfect dinner with cherries jubilee, one of the house specialty desserts. She also received an unexpected present that day, a story that she relished telling, in fun, about how I bought myself a motorcycle on her birthday (I lived with this story until I was able to neutralize it by buying Joni her dream vehicle, a Jeep Wrangler, on my birthday a couple years later).

The following Monday morning, I went to the Department of Motor Vehicles (DMV), picked up a motorcycle exam booklet, read it, returned later that day to take the written test, and easily passed it. Next, I went over to schedule myself for the riding test. To my horror, I learned riding tests were only given two days a week, every other week. The next several sessions were already fully booked. The earliest I could take the test was six weeks away, half way through an Alaskan summer.

My objective was to have my motorcycle license in half that time—reality and my success model did not seem well aligned. While I was filling out the paperwork and paying the fee to register for the motorcycle-riding test, I started asking the woman helping me about other possible options. This was useful because I found out that once you are registered you could go to the test site behind the DMV during any of the scheduled motorcycle-riding tests. If you let the examiner know you are there, you would be able to take the test if someone did not show up, or if the scheduled tests went faster than planned. However, by noting that all the test sessions between now and the week I was scheduled were already over booked, she gave me very little encouragement about being able to take the test early. She also mentioned that an organization called ABATE (**A**laska **B**ikers **A**dvocating **T**raining and **E**ducation) gave a two-day motorcycle rider course sponsored by the motorcycle safety foundation. By taking and passing the ABATE training, all you needed to receive a motorcycle endorsement on your driver's license was show the course certificate to the DMV, pay the fee, and the motorcycle-driving test was waived.

Great, from what seemed like an impossible situation, I now had two options for getting my license earlier. There are always options. All you need to do is decide what you want, when you want it, and then define the pathway that will take you to the desired endpoint.

Before leaving, the clerk at the DMV told me there was a scheduled motorcycle riding examine this coming Wednesday. So on Wednesday, I went to the test site in my car and watched to see what the riding test was like. It included accelerating around right hand and left hand curves with a normal stop, controlled stops on a straight course, emergency stops, emergency sharp turns, and weaving through cones. Now that I knew the sorts of maneuvers I needed to master for my license, I could practice them.

Later when I called ABATE to register for the motorcycle-riding course, I found out their courses were comprehensive, including both classroom and riding instruction, and that they were scheduled every Saturday and Sunday during the summer. The earliest date with an opening was nearly four weeks away. This was closer to my three-week target for getting a license and I decided the training would be worthwhile, especially since I had not ridden a motorcycle for so many years, so I signed up.

During the next two weeks, I practiced riding every day and each day there was improvement. My Valkyrie and I began to work together as a unit. Synchronous. In harmony. In tune with each other. The motorcycle increasingly felt like a part of me. Even though the Valkyrie was long, wide, and heavy, once I got the feel of it, once I learned to coordinate the clutch, gears, and power, once I learned what it liked to do, I found it was as agile as a sports bike.

At the end of two weeks, I felt relaxed riding my Valkyrie around the Anchorage city streets (although I was a bit uncomfortable riding around without a license). There was still much to learn, but I was enjoying every minute of the discovery process. Even though I was not quite ready to take the riding test, my target date for having a license in three weeks was this Saturday, so I decided to go for it. I rode to the DMV on Friday during the motorcycle-riding exam and put my name on the list to take the test. The worst that could happen was that either I would fail or there would not be an opening for me to take the test. In either of these cases, I was already scheduled for the ABATE motorcycle riding course the following week and then I could get my license.

The Thursday evening before the test, I rode to the DMV on my Valkyrie and practiced riding on the test course, repeating all the maneuvers I had seen performed earlier. This was useful as the curves laid out on the asphalt course were sharp, and while I was good at right hand curves, left-handed curves did not feel as natural. I practiced until I was at ease with all aspects of the course, then left.

Friday morning I was at the DMV when the testing started. I gave the examiner my name and went to the side of the course to watch and wait. While watching, I noticed about a third of the people that took the riding test failed. However, those who failed were obviously not comfortable on their motorcycles and they were a menace to themselves and anyone within striking distance. While observing others taking the riding test, I learned the subtleties of what the examiner was looking for. Eventually, there was just myself and two other people waiting on the side of the course. The examiner called a name and one person from the group of two got on his motorcycle and rode over to the test area. I went over to talk with the other person.

"Are you here to take the test?" I asked.

"No, I already have my license; I'm here with my friend who's taking the test now. He just has a learner's permit so I have been riding with him. I rode with him here today since you can't ride alone with just a learner's permit."

He went on to tell me he was a police officer and had been riding motorcycles for 12 years. I thought it was best not to mention I did not have a learner's permit, or that I had been practicing on my own for three weeks, or that I rode over here alone. In fact, I thought it would be a good idea to change the subject.

"I hope your friend passes. He looks confident. I'm sure he will do fine." I said.

I followed with a compliment on his bike, a sure fire way to avoid conversation about anything other than motorcycles. By the time his friend finished the test, I knew everything about his motorcycle, when he got it, where he had ridden it, the accessories he had added, and his plans for the summer.

Then to my surprise, the examiner called my name. Even though the woman at the DMV said this testing session was over booked, the crowd never materialized. I was the last person on the lot, and they had time to do a couple more tests after me, if anyone showed up. This was an example of why you should not base your actions on the views of others (or, for that matter, on views you might have that are based on your own assumptions). More often than not, such views are wrong. The best course of action is to define what you want, how you can get what you want, and go for it. If there are problems, deal with them. There are always going to be problems—no matter what path you choose to take.

"See you around," I said to the police officer, hoping it would not be in any kind of official capacity.

"Good luck," he said and waved as he rode off with his friend.

I took the test, passed it (just barely), rode around to the front of the DMV, parked my Valkyrie, and went inside to get my license. While I was waiting in line, a person next to me asked if I had just passed the motorcycle test. "Yes," I said. I am not sure if it was the leather coat, the helmet, or the Cheshire cat smile on my face that made it obvious, but I did not really care. I was happy.

Even though I had my license, I followed through and took the ABATE Motorcycle riding course, and would strongly recommend a similar course to everyone, regardless of whether you are a first time rider, or someone who has been riding for many years. It teaches street riding strategies, motorcycle handling characteristics, and safety. Their slogan is, "The more you know, the better it gets" and they are right. The following year I took the experienced rider course. The best way to enjoy motorcycle riding is by keeping the rubber side down. A motorcycle safety course (like those sponsored by ABATE) that includes skills development and a refresher of motorcycle riding concepts gives you the knowledge needed to successfully avoid problems and the skills needed to ride with confidence.

The rest of the summer I spent working on perfecting the art of motorcycle riding. On weekdays, I rode after work for at least an hour. On weekends, the rides usually stretched into several hours. One thing about Anchorage in midsummer is that the days are eighteen to twenty hours long. For several weeks around Summer Solstice it is still light at midnight, so after work, and dinner, there is still enough sunlight to enjoy a scenic ride.

I rode every chance I had. I rode my motorcycle from Anchorage along the Turnagan Arm of the Cook Inlet, a road bound by water on one side and cliff bejeweled mountains on the other, or I rode through the Matanuska Valley, with rolling hills and a mountain cut sky. These rides never failed to flood my senses. Feeling, hearing, seeing, smelling, and tasting, damned up, confined by the monotony of sameness, rusted by routine, and rotted by rituals, would burst open, swamping my brain with fresh sensations; the rides scraped away the stagnation and exposed raw nerve endings that danced with newness. While careening down the asphalt ribbon, my skin sparkled as I felt air flow over the contours of my body. When traffic passed from the opposite direction, the air got thick and sloshed around me on all sides, the bigger the vehicle the thicker the air and the more it sloshed. The air spoke to me with a meditative ohmmmmmmme sound, inviting life to pour through my soul. Sight created illusions of motion and motionlessness depending upon where I fixed my gaze. Peering down at my feet the dashed lines on the road were a blur, just in front of my motorcycle the dashes ticked by at a rapid pace, further away they glided slowly toward me, on the horizon their motion was barely perceptible, and distant mountains I rode toward were still. I saw eagles kite in the sky above my head. Air swirled at the base of my full-face helmet ensuring I enjoyed even the briefest scent from a patch of roadside flowers, stagnant water, or dew-laden grass. Yes, there was taste too. Just as a snake darts its tongue in and out, raking information about its surroundings off its surface, when I opened my mouth slightly and quickly pulled air across my tongue a faint taste was noticeable. In the country, the air tasted sweet and mixed with ever changing flavors. In the city, the air tasted sour with a sharp bite or it was dry and chalky. If I was on a country road and the wind was coming toward me from a city, I could taste the city in the air miles before I could see the city itself.

When I ride, my senses are immersed, excited, smothered by the experience. It is a release from tensions, worries, and the routine. It is a sensual experience. It is erotic.

The saddle, the sound, the speed served to focus me on the instant, on the scenery floating by, on risks hiding around every corner, and on skills I needed to hone.

Perfecting the art of motorcycle riding took many hours of practice and I threw myself into the task. I rode by myself. I rode with friends. I rode with local motorcycle-riding clubs. I rode in the Mat-Su Valley bordering the Knik Arm of the Cook Inlet—along the tree and brush encrusted Old Glen Highway following the Knik and Matanuska Rivers, along the curving Fishhook and Bogard Trunk Roads, along the Glenn Highway skirting the Matanuska River to Long Lake passing through places like Sutton, King Mountain, and Chickaloon. I rode along the Turnagain Arm of the Cook Inlet—through towns like Indian, Girdwood, and the mining town of Hope with side stops at the Turnagain House, the Bird Ridge Café and Bakery, the Crow Creek Mine, the Alyeska ski resort, and Portage Glacier.

Occasionally, I took a weekend day and rode to Seward. The road from Anchorage to Seward is one of the most scenic rides in America and Seward is one of the most scenic cities. The city of Seward is located between Resurrection Bay on one side and high mountains on the other side. The mountains jut abruptly up, encircling the Bay, providing a picture-perfect scene in every direction you look.

I rode my Valkyrie passionately during the summer of 1998 and I learned what the Valkyrie liked to do, what its limits were, and what my limits were. The rides continued as the tempera-

CROW CREEK MINE.

Blacksmith's shop and barn. Constructed in 1898.

Mess Hall, also built in 1898.

Turnagain Arm of the Cook Inlet.

Deep snow in pass near Summit Lake.

Kenai Lake.

Exit Glacier.

Resurrection Bay as seen from the Town of Seward.

Traditional Athabascan grave houses or spirit houses.

Alaskan Native Totem.

Moss encrusted boots.

Bridge crossing the Knik River.

TRIP AROUND ANCHORAGE AREA.

Hand built Siberian prayer chapel.

Old St. Nicholas Russian Orthodox Church.

Evening visit of a bull moose in our backyard.

Turquoise glacial ice floating in Portage Lake.

The Igloo, half way between Anchorage and Fairbanks, is a well-known landmark along the Parks Highway.

Skinny Dick's Halfway Inn between Nenana and Fairbanks.

Ester Gold Camp Hotel and Restaurant.

The historic gold rush era Malemute Saloon.

ANCHORAGE TO DELTA JUNCTION.

Alaskan mosquito (burl art).

Delta Junction, Alaska – Northern terminus of the "ALCAN Highway".

BEAVER CREEK TO WHITEHORSE.

Glacial silt
blowing across
Kluane Lake.

Abandoned town of
Silver City.

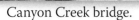

Canyon Creek bridge.

Whitehorse bed and breakfast.

Buffalo outside Whitehorse.

WHITEHORSE TO DAWSON CITY.

Fox Lake fire convoy
checkpoint.

Montague roadhouse ruins.

Old flat-bottom riverboat
at Pelly Crossing.

Five Fingers Rapids on the
Yukon River.

Arrival at the Klondike River.

tures dropped and the leaves turned golden. Then, when it began to freeze, I reluctantly put my motorcycle away for the winter.

When you do a lot of motorcycle riding, you learn a lot about riding motorcycles. However, by being in action, by doing, you also learn a lot about life. Early in my riding, I learned that if I fixed my attention on a danger in the road (a hole, a branch, a rock, some gravel), and concentrated on the danger while trying to maneuver around it, I would hit the obstacle. However, if I saw an obstacle in the road and looked at the path required to avoid the danger, then I would miss it. When riding a motorcycle, you look where you want to go because you go where you are looking. The same is true in life. You always go in the direction you are looking. You are at any moment where you are now, this instant, because of what you were concentrating on in the past. Your decisions, your actions, what you were focusing on, all brought you to where you are today.

*　*　*　*　*

I was on the threshold of a new life. Passion moved me from a place where having a motorcycle was just a thought, to a place where motorcycling was an intimate part of my being. This transition had a significant impact on me, a life changing impact, but I would not fully realize the magnitude or direction of this change for over a year.

Thinking Radically Creates Possibilities

"I work at being optimistic about life. Pessimism, certainly cynicism, is an enemy. Those things destroy possibilities. Optimism is the right outlook to have. I'm convinced it creates possibilities."

TOMMY LEE JONES

Alice laughed. "There's no use trying," she said, "One can't believe impossible things."

"I dare say you haven't had much practice," said the Queen, "When I was your age I did it for half-an-hour a day. Why, sometimes I've believed as many as six impossible things before breakfast."

LEWIS CARROLL

"The only way to discover the limits of the possible is to go beyond them into the impossible."

ARTHUR C. CLARKE

"My interest in life comes from setting myself huge, apparently unachievable challenges and trying to rise above them." "I firmly believe that anything is possible."

RICHARD BRANSON

Snow and ice covered the roads in Anchorage, but the bitter cold of an Alaskan winter was incapable of cooling the burning passion I had for riding motorcycles. The fire within continued with its ravenous appetite. Driven by the wind, mere forces of nature could not reduce the intensity of the blaze.

Flames were consuming me, so I fed them by reading motorcycle magazines. However, my compulsion led me to devour the latest issues within a few days. Then there was a long, empty, dry wait for the next editions to arrive at the newsstands. To fill the void I began reading books on motorcycling—motorcycle riding techniques, motorcycle novels, motorcycle catalogs, an encyclopedia of motorcycles, and motorcycle travel guides.

Around mid-January, I ran out of books. It is incredible that you can go into any bookstore and find shelf after shelf of books on golfing, or boating, or cooking. However, there is a scarcity of motorcycling adventure books. I went into two national megabookstores and could only find a couple dozen books on something as fundamentally important, as critical to one's survival, as basic a need as motorcycling (interesting in light of the fact that motorcycle sales are growing exponentially). The market for motorcycle books is undoubtedly poised to ignite, but this vision of the future gave me little comfort now.

I came to the realization that I had entered a desert, an arid region where motorcycling in the mental, the spiritual, and the physical sense was devoid of life, a desolate area that would remain barren until mid-April when the streets and highways were free of snow and ice, and I could ride again. While mid-April was three months away, it seemed like forever, because the fire was consuming me.

I decided to call my brother Lloyd, in hope of some relief. Naturally, the conversation quickly moved to motorcycles.

"Wouldn't it be great to get together sometime for a ride?" I said.

"Yeah, maybe I could ship my motorcycle from Seattle to

Anchorage on the ferry and we could do some riding this summer," Lloyd replied.

This was the seed of a great idea, a thought that deserved a leap into the sublime world of radical thinking, a time to stretch for something grand.

"Hey Lloyd, why not ship your bike up to Anchorage, we could ride down the Alaska Highway to Seattle together, and then I could ship my Valkyrie back. Or better yet, I could ride down to Seattle with you then turn around and ride my Valkyrie back to Anchorage. What a magnificent adventure that would be."

Extraordinary. Clouds of hope burst open, pouring water upon the wasteland, and the desert began to blossom. It could easily take three months to research and plan this trip. We would need to decide on the route, develop a list of essential gear and supplies, and read about the many historical towns and interesting sights along the Alaska Highway. Here was a future I could clearly see, a daring exploit, a place I wanted to be, and a challenge deserving of the effort. We decided to discuss the idea with our wives and see if there were any showstoppers. If things looked good, we would do it.

When I mentioned the idea to Joni, she was totally behind it. She had been planning to buy me a cross-country motorcycle tour package for my birthday and agreed this would be even better. I could spend time with my brother and go on a great cross-country motorcycle ride too. Incredibly, Joni already had a similar idea. Her insights are uncannily on the mark and she is always supportive of the people around her. While Joni cannot ride a motorcycle because of back problems, there are things she does that I cannot do, and there are things we love to do together. Love is about growing while together and apart, appreciating differences, and nurturing common ground. I know I am lucky to have Joni as a best friend and life companion; times like this just reinforced how wonderful a person she is.

Immediately after getting two thumbs up, I dove into the project spending several days putting together a draft plan. I found a map that covered Alaska, the Yukon Territory, and British Colombia, and outlined a possible route to Seattle and back. I calculated the mileage between stops and then estimated how long the trip would take (assuming 275 to 350 miles a day so we would have time to visit interesting places along the way). Next, I bought some travel guides on Canada to learn about country entrance and exit requirements. Then I started putting together a preliminary list of things to bring on the trip, which included clothes, tools, camping equipment, first aid supplies, emergency items, and miscellaneous things like a camera, journal, and CB radio.

I e-mailed Lloyd the information I had put together for comments. However, without waiting for a reply, I continued to aggressively take the steps required to turn this idea into a reality. I was enjoying being involved with a motorcycle related activity (especially since it was the middle of winter in Alaska) and continued reading, gathering information, and refining details. Lloyd and I periodically talked on the phone and exchanged e-mail messages about the trip. Then, one day during a telephone conversation, Lloyd mentioned that he had just accepted a job in San Antonio, Texas, and would be starting work a couple of months before our planned ride. As we continued to talk, it appeared under the circumstances a joint motorcycle trip this year would not be possible.

After hanging up the phone, I sat back to reflect on what had just happened. It was strange, because things had changed externally but not internally. The trip as defined moments earlier no longer existed, but I was still totally committed. Therefore, to bring the trip back to life I would need to redefine it, recreate it, and embrace the change as an exciting opportunity waiting to be seized, cultivated, and nourished. This would be an epic trip, a once-in-a-lifetime adventure that would immerse me in majestic scenery and take me to places steeped in history, and I refused to let the dream die. 1998 was a centennial year of the gold rush era in the Northwest Territories (1897/98), and like the cheechakos during the Klondike stampede, an unknown force pulled me toward the adventure, the challenge, and the dreams of a wild and untamed land.

I decided to try to find someone else to go with me. If the effort to find a traveling companion failed, I still planned to go on the trip. If I ended up making the journey alone, it would just add a new dimension to the adventure. A solo trip would be an adventure within an adventure, a personal and mental challenge far beyond what I had previously considered, and a riveting adventure that would test me in ways I had never been tested before. My commitment was not only unchanged, it was intensified. My passion was hurling me through what might have been a major obstacle. Radical thinking was helping to push me through the boundaries of defeat into the exciting realm of unlimited possibilities.

Over the next several weeks, I discussed the motorcycle trip I was planning with neighbors, friends at work, and people

I knew at various motorcycle and accessory shops. Many were interested and would have liked to go, but no one could make the trip work for them at this time. I continued to make inquiries, and it would have been great if someone decided to go along at the last moment, but I began to assume this was going to be a solo adventure.

Riding alone was a significant planning assumption. The potential for breakdowns or injuries in the remote country I would be traveling through required a greater consideration of survival issues, because I would no longer be able to rely on someone else in case of trouble. I began to consider all the possible problems that might be encountered during the trip, and how I could effectively respond to each one, given the limited space to pack "stuff" on my motorcycle.

Going solo also presented an opportunity to expand my thinking, to redefine the route, and to take an unconstrained view on what would make an exceptional trip. I decided to see as many new places as possible by not retracing my path on the return trip, and to spend time with my parents and some of my family while in Washington State. After researching the possibilities, I selected the route shown on the map on the next page. My trip outline indicated this would work within the three-weeks of vacation I could take from work. The trip now had a focus in terms of both path and aspirations. Tactics were continually refined and improved upon, up to the time I actually started on the journey. A journey was waiting that was saturated with many exciting physical and mental challenges.

I managed to survive until April. The flames were fed by immersing myself in the trip planning details, so I was not con-

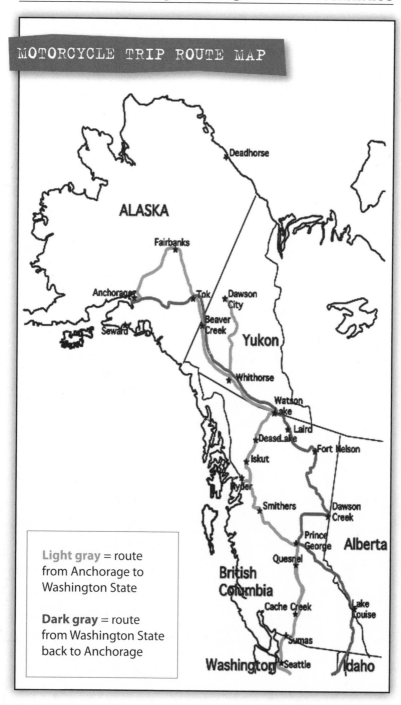

MOTORCYCLE TRIP ROUTE MAP

Light gray = route from Anchorage to Washington State

Dark gray = route from Washington State back to Anchorage

sumed. Even though snow was still spotty in the valleys and deep through the mountain passes, the highways and streets in and around Anchorage were finally ice-free. I was able to ride again, to transform motorcycling from the mental back to the physical. I rode every chance I had. I rode for the pure enjoyment of riding, for the freedom and the wind, but I also rode to hone the techniques required during my cross-country trip that would begin on July 3.

By this time I had a clear vision of my trip, what skills I needed to acquire, and the types of challenges I faced. I knew how I wanted to touch the future, and the impacts I wanted this trip to have on my life. I wanted to use the trip to stimulate my mind, invigorate my body, and build a foundation for a book I hoped someday to have the time to write. I wanted this trip to be the start of something new in my life. I wanted it to be the dream I had, and lived. What I did not yet realize was that this trip would touch my future in unexpected ways. The impact on my life would result in a fundamental change in direction. A change that I yearned for but that I thought, at this time, was impossible to achieve. By living one dream, I became compelled to live other dreams. It was not a step; it was a leap into an unforeseen and wonderful world of change that I savor to this day.

Over the next couple of months I rode with three objectives in mind: (1) to expand my comfort with riding my Valkyrie cruiser on different road surfaces (asphalt, dirt, gravel, rock, and mud), (2) to build my endurance by learning how to be relaxed and comfortable on long rides, and (3) to teach myself to see interesting things along the road.

My first objective required that I ride on as many challenging road surfaces as possible. I already had one summer of riding my Valkyrie; however, I had not yet taken it onto dirt, mud, rock, or gravel roads. All these road conditions are prevalent along the Alaskan and Cassiar highways, which are two of the main north-south roads in western Canada. To fill this gap in my experience, I began to take side trips, which in Alaska usually results in the disappearance of an asphalt surface.

One day I called Jim, a fellow motorcycling enthusiast, to see if he was up to a road trip. Jim had a sweet-looking sporty candy apple red Kawasaki Vulcan and always appreciated an excuse for a ride. We hooked up and rode from Anchorage to Girdwood, along the base of the rugged Chugach Mountains skirting the edge of the scenic Turnagain Arm of the Cook Inlet, then down a three-mile road to the historic Crow Creek Gold Mine. The road to the mine was a narrow, winding, rocky, rut-infested, dirt and mud road. Just what I was hoping for. Jim led the way. His motorcycle was right at home in this environment. To me, dirt, mud, and rocks seemed to be an unnatural surface for a cruiser, but as I pushed myself to keep up with Jim, I found my Valkyrie liked the off-pavement action. There was not a problem with my motorcycle on this type of road; the only problem was in my mind.

When we arrived at the mine site entrance, we found it was open to the public. For a nominal fee, you could visit the original mining camp and pan for gold in Crow Creek. Seven original buildings, built in 1898, were still standing: the blacksmith's shop, barn, icehouse, commissary, mine owners cabin, mess hall, meat cache, and bunkhouse. The Crow Creek Mine is still operational, however, the original camp is now a National Historic Site, and the family responsible for its preservation lives and works there with no telephone, electricity, or running water (excluding the creek during the summer months).

Visiting the Crow Creek mining camp was like stepping through a portal to the past. The well-maintained buildings, filled with antiques, are located in a picturesque valley setting. Panning for gold and actually finding gold flakes in my pan was exhilarating. You may not leave there wealthy. In fact, the gold I found did not even cover the entrance fee, but it was gold panned in Alaska, and I still have several small flakes as a memento of the experience.

When we left the mine, the road we exited on seemed friendlier than the one we came on (even though it was the same road). Jim and I raced back to Girdwood, alternating the lead. At about 40 mph, the ruts pulled the motorcycle away from our seats and the muddy spots caused the rear end to float sideways or fishtail as the bikes wallowed through them. It was fascinating to learn that my Valkyrie was so versatile; that my motorcycle was limited only by what I thought was possible, that it was me that constrained its performance. When I let it free, and when I freed my mind of limits, the motorcycle and I performed in harmony with whatever environment we were in.

Because bad roads would be a big part of my cross-country trip through the northern wilderness, doing some riding off paved roads for the first time produced a major increase in my confidence regarding this aspect of the trip.

My second objective was to build endurance. In order to learn the art of long distance motorcycling I took three trips to

Seward (a round trip from Anchorage of 250 miles). The scenery along this road was breathtaking and seemed to change every time I rode it. The first time I went was in late April. Going over the pass between Anchorage and Seward, there were still several feet of snow covering everything except the black asphalt road that had been dried by the spring sun. It was strange to ride a motorcycle through that winter wonderland. It was like being in a picture postcard. There were snowcapped peaks, reflective roadside lakes, rustic cabins in leafless forests, and snow machines that raced along beside the road. During the next trip, melting snow had given birth to numerous waterfalls and rivulets along the stone cliffs and sloping hills next to the road. On the third trip, the birch trees were full of leaves and the meadows were green and spotted with wild flowers, including the ever-present fireweed.

It surprised me how much there was to learn about long-distance riding. At the end of my first 250-mile ride (Anchorage-Seward-Anchorage), I had tired hands, a strained back, and cramped legs. When I finally got back to Anchorage and climbed off my motorcycle, I could hardly walk. I felt like a cowboy after being in the saddle all day. During the second ride, I taught myself how to sit up straight, change position periodically, and stretch as I was riding. On the third trip, I was still very relaxed at the end of the ride. In fact, I felt good enough to do the trip again that same day. I am glad I gave myself this experience. If I had just headed down the Alaskan highway without first acquiring the long-distance riding skills I needed, going the planned 300 to 400 miles a day would have resulted in not enjoying several days of the trip while I was getting broken in.

The third objective was to teach myself to see interesting things along the road. Once I am on the road, I have an awful habit of just wanting to get to where I am going. The objective of my upcoming trip was not to get somewhere. After all, I was starting and ending the trip in Anchorage. My objective was to maximize the experience so it was important to make myself stop, explore, and learn something about the places I was to pass through. I also wanted flexibility rather than rigidity, so I needed to be willing to take alternate routes, explore side roads, and open myself up to investigating interesting things I saw along the way.

There are numerous opportunities to explore historic sites or scenic parks near Anchorage. During short trips, I visited many areas of interest and learned the benefits of enriching my rides by immersing myself in the culture and history of the area I rode through. I now find that the stops, the conversations with people, the history, and the culture are jewels that sparkle in the mind long after the blur of the road is gone. Here are a few of the jewels I found near Anchorage.

The Eklutna Historic Park is located in an Athabascan Native Village, about 30 miles outside Anchorage, just off the Glenn Highway. Inside the park is the original St. Nicholas Russian Orthodox Church, a hand built Siberian prayer chapel, and spirit houses (native grave sites) painted with each family's traditional clan colors. The park is rich in early native Alaskan memorabilia including old photographs, native artifacts, and buildings.

The Hatcher Pass road is north of Palmer, off the main highway. It follows streams and passes through high country meadows on the way to the Independence Mine Historical Park, located 70 miles north of Anchorage. The last 9 miles of road to the mine is gravel and dirt. There are several old buildings and numerous pieces of equipment remaining from gold mining operations during the period from 1938 to 1941. The view from the mine is spectacular and the ruins are heavy with the history of the early gold rush days.

Between the southernmost portion of the Hatcher Pass Road and Wasilla is the Wasilla-Fishhook Road, a wonderful twisting countryside road weaves through the rolling hills that fall away from the pass. It is a challenging ride on a motorcycle; it gives you an opportunity to test yourself, to reach for the edge, and to find and experience your limits.

Portage Glacier is 55 miles southeast of Anchorage near the end of the Turnagain Arm of the Cook Inlet. Glaciers speckle the road leading to Portage Glacier, and Portage Lake was filled with large turquoise-blue icebergs floating in it. The visitor's center has a wonderful educational movie about glaciers. In addition to hiking on and around the glaciers, you can also go on an ice worm safari. Yes, ice worms really do exist. They are small black worms found, at certain times, in the glacier fields. Hiking on the glacier was an unexpected adventure with serpentine streams formed by snowmelt, turquoise ice caves, bottomless crevasses, and glacier lakes.

I now cherish the riches of both the journey, and the stops along the way.

The stops are like a magnifying glass on life. They allow me a chance to see the small details, to learn the history of a place, to experience its culture, to meet the people, and to linger in a moment isolated from, yet connected to, every other moment, everywhere on earth. It is a step off the whirl of life, allowing me to become saturated with the timelessness of a place and a moment.

The journey, on the other hand, is a refreshing swim in a raging river of time. It is a perilous path with white-water, swift currents, and plunging falls. It never ceases to excite. On a motorcycle, the journey is a sensuous experience that totally immerses me in the world, fully stimulating my senses, and awakening my mind. While on a motorcycle, I have an unobstructed panoramic view of the road, the sky, the trees, the cliffs, the glaciers, the eagles, and the moose. Motion is an illusion. When the path is straight, wide, and clear, and I ride directly toward a mountain abruptly piercing the landscape in front of me, I feel as though I am floating, suspended in time, motionless. When the path narrows and twists through tunnels of trees, shrubbery, and hills, speed is magnified and I feel as though I am transporting through time and that the motorcycle is an extension of my body responding to my every thought—it must respond to thought, because there is no time to react. While riding, I can smell a nearby lake, burning leaves, and pine trees. The sun caresses my body. The wind massages my skin and whispers in my ears, and my Valkyrie tells me by its throaty growl if it is relaxed or it is working to respond to my command. No other experience touches the senses as profoundly as motorcycling, and its addiction, once submitted to, is tenacious.

*   *   *   *   *

In one month, my adventure was to begin, and I was already anticipating the experience with excitement. The route was decided, the departure date was defined (July 3), and essential riding skills were developed. A few remaining details included clearing up work-related issues before leaving on vacation, pre-trip maintenance on my Valkyrie, buying special equipment, and getting new tires. In addition to necessary camping gear, personal items, and clothing, I also defined supplies required during the solo trip to deal with the possibility of a flat tire, illness, a breakdown, an accident or injury, and weather extremes.

The future was certain, because when the seed of this idea was planted, I began to visualize what the success case looked like, to think from the future, and to build a path of actions back to the moment. The approach of planning from the desired endpoint to the present is radical but very powerful (backwards planning). This is done by defining when you wish to achieve an aspiration, then stepping back one time step (a week, a month, or a year, as appropriate) and defining where you need to be at that point in time, and continuing to step backwards from your aspiration until you have arrived at the starting point—today. This approach is the opposite of how most people plan, which is to start from today and define the steps needed to get to an endpoint (forward planning). Forward planning is a weak approach.

Here is one example, from my life, showing the significant difference in results realized when using the two approaches (forward and backward planning). At age thirty-five, I decided I wanted to retire when I was fifty-five. I projected my salary and expenses into the future and found that with social security, a company pension, and company health benefits, my wife and I could not live the way we wanted to live, even if we retired at age 65. By significantly cutting our expenses, which meant years of a dreary life style, and by my wife and I both working, we could improve our retirement income but those extreme actions had little impact on reducing our retirement age from 65.

After learning the power of backwards planning, I applied the concept to the problem of retiring by age 55. I retired at age 50.

These planning processes seem similar on the surface, but forward planning is weak because it most often defines a failure case (a case that falls short of the aspiration), it highlights reasons why extraordinary results are not possible, and it frustrates you by focusing your attention on incremental changes that have little impact on the outcome. In contrast, backwards planning is powerful in showing you how to achieve extraordinary results because the approach defines a success case (because you start your planning from where you want to be, and when you want to be there), it helps you to identify where you need to focus your efforts, and it illuminates possibilities for closing gaps between where you are now and where you want to be.

Planning is an important element for achieving significant goals in your life, and I find that improvement principles from life, such as planning, apply equally well to enhancing motor-cycle-riding skills. Truth is truth.

When you are traveling down a winding country road (life), you decide if this is a scenic ride (I will retire whenever it happens) or a ride on the edge (I will retire at age fifty-five). If you wish to test yourself, to find the limit of what is possible, to know the full capability of yourself, the capability of the road you are on, and the capability of your motorcycle (something I refer to as the capability of the man-road-machine interface), then you do not want a scenic ride, you want a ride on the edge. A ride on the edge is where you challenge your limits. If you have a passion for the edge, if you push to discover your true limits, you will consistently exceed your expectations and go beyond what you imagine as possible.

Forward planning is like riding in a dense fog. Your focus is on what is right in front of you, you must ride slowly in case there is danger in the road, and limited visibility means you are unable to see shortcuts or alternative routes.

Planning from where you are now, the present, into the future (forward planning) will not allow you to ride through a curve on the edge because looking down the road from where you are leads to a hopeless loop of confusion. As you approach the curve, thinking from the present requires you to first decide where to start braking, then how long to decelerate, then where to begin your turn, then whether to take an inside or outside path. If you then, while looking at the future, discover that you are approaching a blind corner, and your actions were lining you up to hug the centerline, you have set yourself up for the wrong approach into the blind corner. In planning from the present, you find that the decisions you make often result in outcomes that are inconsistent with the future you are heading into, you will become hopelessly lost in a trial and error solution to the section of road you are on, and you will set yourself up to experience many needless failures. In addition, since you are consuming all your energy and attention on a continuous stream of readjustments and changes to your plan, you will not have the energy or attention left to stretch yourself. You will undershoot your full potential, the full potential of your bike, and the capability of the road you are on. You will miss the edge.

Thinking from the future eliminates the need to attempt to find the best solution by trial and error while you are speeding down the road. To ride on the edge you must look as far down the road as possible and backward plan. When you are approaching a turn, you plan from the furthest point into the turn you can see, back to where you are now. You think from the future, not from the present, and definitely not from the past. By thinking from the future, you will determine what it will take to optimize your performance at each point along the road, and this will allow you to successfully negotiate the turn at the limit of the man-road-machine interface—it will allow you to ride on the edge.

By looking at the curve (the future), then examining the characteristics of the curve (whether it is a blind corner, or a corner with good visibility and no traffic), you can determine whether to take an outside or an inside path through the curve. Defining the path through the curve will determine when you need to start turning the motorcycle, which will determine the speed you need to be going at that point, which will determine when you need to start braking. Therefore, you have defined the required actions between you and the curve. By using this strategy, you know in advance what you need to do at each point along the path. This knowledge will allow you time to focus on other things like uncertainties (wind, oncoming traffic, animals along the road, and road conditions) and improving your performance.

To ride on the edge you must plan from the future to the present.

Because the path to your dream is different from any other path you might be on, a kaleidoscope of change (curves in the road) will entertain you along the way. Embrace change as stepping-stones to where you want to be, purge fear from your mind, keep your objectives clear, and maintain an unwavering commitment. As you travel down the path, make each step an opportunity to improve on the trip, to make it better, to keep your dream new and vital.

Some people prefer a straight road while others go out and look for roads with lots of curves. When riding on the edge, a curve in the road is not something to fear, it is a wonderful experience. A curve clearly defines your next challenge and it is the most exhilarating part of the road. This is where you grow, where you learn to improve your skills, and where you become more confident with facing challenges. A curve in the road is a free learning experience.

Needless fear can prevent you from taking maximum advantage of a learning opportunity such as a curve in the road. One thing that might hold you back is a concern with falling. A scary thought about falling can keep you from achieving the exhilaration of a high performance corner, it can prevent you from reaching the limit of the man-road-machine interface, and it can deter you from riding on the edge.

If you decide to ride a motorcycle, you must admit that you could fall off. If you ride a motorcycle a lot, falling is an activity you will likely get a chance to experience, so you must be objective and honest with yourself about that possibility. The critical factor here is acknowledging the possibility so you can get the scary stuff out in the open, deal with it, put it out of your mind, and focus on the ride.

To enjoy the sport of motorcycling you must do everything possible to minimize the potential for a fall—learn the handling characteristics of your motorcycle and learn how to drive defensively. Nobody wants to fall off a motorcycle, but opening up yourself to the possibility is an important part of preparing for that situation and dealing with it so you can focus on the more important elements related to learning to ride on the edge.

If you have watched a high-speed motorcycle race, you may have seen a person fall at over 100 mph, get up, and walk away without any breaks or abrasions. After seeing something like this, you immediately realize that the fear you have of falling is much worse than the reality of what actually happened when the professional rider fell. Once you know that you can fall and come out all right, falling is no longer something that you need to fear. The secret is wearing good equipment (helmet and leathers) and relaxing if you fall (tensing causes injuries and broken bones).

Professional motorcycle racers are mentally and physically prepared for a fall, and as a result, they do not need to waste valuable time and energy worrying about falling. Instead, they focus on winning the race.

Embrace the curves in the road; this is where the excitement is. Do not focus on falling, focus on successfully negotiating the curve. This is the most efficient approach because it takes more energy to keep something from happening than it takes to make something happen.

If you do fall, you are just breaking in your leathers. If you are not willing to fall, do not ride.

Next, it is important to have a clear view of what your objectives are as you travel down the road toward your dream. A common mistake some people make in planning is failing to keep the true challenge in mind. This can cause you to unknowingly waste time and energy. If you are riding down a country road with someone else, remain focused on the challenges of the road, not on the other rider. In contrast to commonly held beliefs, focusing on matching or beating the other rider actually interferes with your ability to find the limit of the man-road-machine interface; it makes it nearly impossible to ride on the edge.

If you have the wrong objective in mind, you will succeed in the wrong thing. When focusing on the other rider, you will constantly play catch up. The other rider imagined as the competitor will affect how hard you try. You will be focused on their limits rather than your limits and you will believe you have succeeded when you are able to maintain or beat their pace. By using the other rider as a model for your performance, you are constraining yourself. When the rider takes an inside path through a curve, you will take the same path with the idea of trying to improve on their performance. However, it might be that an outside path is the fastest way through the curve, it might be significantly faster, but you missed the opportunity by concentrating on the wrong objective—the other rider. If you remain focused on the true objective of pushing yourself to the limit, then you will find opportunities to significantly improve upon the performance of the other rider.

Once you have defined your course of action by looking to the future and working back to the present, once you have analyzed your fears and put them behind you, and once you have a clear view of the objectives, then burn your bridges. Fully commit to the plan and do not define alternatives. I am not saying to never change your plan (you should always look for ways to improve); what I am saying is that you can only have one plan. An alternative plan distracts, shatters confidence, and allows for a way out—an excuse for failing. Commitment minimizes distractions. The magic of commitment is that it frees you up to succeed.

Finally, once you go through a curve, assess what you have learned so you can apply this learning to the next curve in the road. By doing this you will continuously improve, and you will become comfortable facing other challenges encountered during your ride.

*   *   *   *   *

I was transforming all the reading and practicing for the trip into living the dream. The dream itself took root in passion during mid-January, then came the genuine belief that it was possible (I did not know why I could not do it), radical thinking created exceptional opportunities, and finally I committed myself to the dream regardless of any problems I encountered. I was nearing the moment of doing. The challenge was clearly defined and I was dedicated to succeeding. Planning and preparation was integrated with performance.

The achievement of any goal consists of a continuous cycle of thought and action, bridged by ideas and plans. Therefore, while I always write my plans down, I never write a plan in stone.

Instead, I define a path forward. When I see an opportunity to improve my plan, I make changes along the way. Improvements have no limits so flexibility is of key importance.

Flexibility was certainly important during the development of the list of equipment needed for the solo motorcycle journey through remote, desolate, and unforgiving country. I started out with a simple list consisting of mainly clothes and camping gear. Then as I read magazine articles and books about motorcycle trips and as I talked about this trip with various people, the list was modified and refined.

Everything I took had to fit into leather saddlebags attached to each side of my Valkyrie. I also bought a T-Bag, which is a custom-made motorcycle pack with a pocket designed to fit over the sissy seat pad. The T-Bag can mount on the luggage rack over the rear wheel, to accommodate a passenger, or sit on the passenger seat when riding solo. When mounted to sit on the passenger seat, it makes a great backrest during long rides and this is the way I mounted it. You can also mount a roll bag on the top of the T-Bag for carrying a sleeping bag. The capacity of both saddlebags was 1.5 cubic feet, the T-Bag was 2.0 cubic feet, and the roll bag was 0.5 cubic feet. for a total capacity of 4 cubic feet. (a capacity equivalent to a cube that is 19 inches on each side). One lingering challenge was how to pack everything required into the limited space and weight constraints associated with traveling on a motorcycle.

A few weeks before my scheduled departure date on July 3, 1998, I decided to pack everything I had assembled for the trip to see how it would fit into the available space. To my dismay, all my bags were full and I had packed fewer than half the items on my list. It was obvious that aggressive steps would have to be taken to reduce the load without sacrificing either safety or a reasonable degree of comfort.

I explored a local mountaineering store for some help since mountain climbers have a similar space and weight problems during their trips. I went high tech for the tent (a two-man mountaineering tent that folded down into a very compact bag and only weighed 3.5 pounds), ground pad (self-inflating), one-burner butane stove, cooking and eating utensils, ring dry towel, thermal underwear (Duofold Polyester which is warmer and has half the bulk of cotton) and collapsible water bottles. I also bought a variety of nylon stuff bags that I highly recommend for organizing and compacting the contents of a pack. By tightly rolling bulky items like clothing and putting them in stuff bags, you can further minimize space. Next, I put together a minimal travel first aid kit designed by a doctor. The contents of the first aid kit fit into a fanny pack, which made it very compact, and if needed it could be strapped around my waist rather than having to carry around an awkward first aid box. Finally, I went through the list eliminating bulky clothing and ruthlessly cutting everything that was not essential.

Once again, I laid everything out on the floor and started packing the bags. Success! It all fit into the available 4 cubic foot space. This was a great thing to do before going on the road because it allowed me to think about how it all needed to go together. For example, several things need to be quickly accessible like the tire gauge, camera, logbook, first aid kit, windshield cleaner, and sunglasses. Also, the last thing I want to do during a rainstorm is tear open my bag and get everything wet, so I put all my rain gear in a stuff bag and placed it on the top inside my right saddlebag. The following is the final list of the supplies I took. Yes, it all fit inside a four cubic foot space.

CAMPING GEAR	CLOTHING	MISC. ITEMS
two man tent	2 pairs of jeans	Buck knife & case
ground pad	4 pairs of socks	3 flares
sleeping bag	4 pairs underwear	1 qt. motor oil
1-burner stove	fleece jacket	tire puncture sealant
1 can butane	thermal underwear	tire pump
1 bowl	fleece neckband	tire repair kit
fork/spoon/knife	tennis shoes	1 set spare fuses
1-qt. cook pot	bathing suit	tire pressure gauge
scrub pad	4 short sleeve shirts	set of motorcycle tools
towel	3 long sleeve shirts	small vise grips
bar of soap	kidney belt	motorcycle alarm
sm bag toiletries	cold weather gloves	2 spark plugs
matches (waterproof)	hat	windshield cleaning kit
first-aid kit	reading glasses	diary and pen
liquid camp soap	sun glasses	camera & 6 rolls film
motorcycle cover	Gore-Tex raincoat	tape recorder & tapes
flashlight & batteries	Gore-Tex rain pants	6 ft rubber hose
hand cleaning wipes	boot Gators	chain/lock (Kryptonite)
2 2-qt water bottles	rain gloves	2 saddlebag inserts
light rope		4 bungee cords
paper towels		cell phone & charger
zip ties		CB radio
maps		safety wire
emergency food		duct/elec./clear tapes
Swiss Army knife		6 leather cords

Motorcycle supplies taken on the trip though Alaska, the Yukon Territory, British Columbia, Alberta, Washington State, and Idaho.

A Public Stand Increases Commitment

"The secret of life is to have a task, something you devote your entire life to, something you bring everything to, every minute of the day for your whole life. And the most important thing is—it must be something you cannot possibly do!"

HENRY MOORE

"If one advances confidently in the direction of his dreams, and endeavors to live the life which he has imagined, he will meet with success unexpected in common hours."

HENRY DAVID THOREAU

AY 1

The day before the journey was to begin, I did a last check on my motorcycle and supplies, and shortly after 10:00 p.m., Joan and I went to bed. We talked for a few minutes then lay silently together. Joni's warmth, her gentle touches, her loving ways, made the edges of silhouetted bedroom furnishings seem to glow like crystalline beads of dew on a single silky web glistening in the early morning sun. The glow pulsed around the outline of the bed frame, the dresser, the door, and radiated from the corners of the room. It slowly spread. The crystalline beads brightened. They sparkled. A sparkle like fireworks going off inside bubbles of freshly poured vintage champagne, a frothy foam of light with spheres forming and bursting frantically along the sides of fluted glass. The sparkle lasted for a brief moment—an infinite moment. A moment where fragrances permeate still air, and the subtle perfume releases seconds that last forever. Motionlessly we basked in the heat radiating between us. Then, breaking the quietness she said, "Have a good trip but be safe and come back in one piece." I pushed the side of my head into the pillow and let the thick mellowness of the moment succumb to a deeply restful state that lingered until unconsciousness took its place.

The alarm went off at 6:00 a.m., instantly transforming night into day, and I desperately gasped for consciousness. It was July 3, the day I had been preparing for, the day I had been anticipating during the past five and a half months. I was about to begin a three-week motorcycle journey that would weave itself through a wonderland of pristine vistas, a country that barely notices man's footsteps, where nature is unspoiled, and animals regard humans as an oddity—a curiosity to be watched quietly so as not to frighten them away.

Thoughts of both excitement and trepidation raced through my mind. Books I had read and people I had talked to about the country I would be going through related stories of incidents where people were maimed or killed in bear attacks, stories of nearly impassable roads, and stories of those stranded in the middle of an uninhabited and hostile wilderness. However, the same books, the same people, also tell of abundant wildlife, incredible scenery, and the friendliness of people in the North

Country. I was prepared for the many uncertainties associated with a solo trip, but at the same time, I expected the best experience possible and was ready to plunge into the journey, to taste the luxury of an untouched land. This was going to be a great life adventure and I was prepared to live it, to immerse myself in it, to splash in its richness.

After my shower, I went downstairs and looked out the kitchen window. There had been sunshine during the past several days. However, that morning, the day of my departure, it was raining. It was a gentle, fine, misty rain, the kind where droplets are barely visible and fall softly upon the skin. The droplets floated from the sky in close formation, forming airy sheets of water that gradually saturated everything it covered. Surfaces looked like a chilled glass in a steamy sauna where water droplets form, pool together and then run down the side.

Briefly, I was disheartened about having to begin my journey in the rain, but quickly my mood shifted to the waiting venture. I was prepared for this, and fully expected there would be days when it would rain. This was just an opportunity to test my rain gear. A chance to try it out, to see if it worked before distance grew between me and a Wal-Mart store. An occasion to evaluate my foul weather gear before entering that shopless world I was hoping to find where necessities of life can be purchased, but little more.

Joni and I ate breakfast together, then I loaded my Valkyrie with the supplies I had organized the night before. Joni came out into the garage to take pictures of my preparations and departure. She was a bit quiet, and I could tell that while she still fully supported me in this adventure, she was a little worried.

Joni has a quiet confidence about herself, and when she gets worried, she just places the situation in God's hands and surrenders her worries to Him.

She watched as I completed preparations for the trip, which included checking and adjusting the load, donning my Gore-Tex rain gear, climbing onto my motorcycle in the rain, and posing for one final picture as I got ready to leave. Joni was happy for me. If it were not for the fact that she had five back operations, and her body was no longer motorcycle-friendly, she would be coming along on her own bike. Since she was staying behind, she made the departure ceremonious. She always makes special occasions extra special for people. Her smile was the last thing I saw as I drove off. Even though she was not physically on the ride, I carried that smile with me during the entire trip.

One thing I had forgotten to do earlier was to fill my motorcycle with gasoline; so, shortly after pulling onto the Parks Highway (Alaska Highway 1), I stopped at a Mapco station on the edge of town, and filled the 5.3-gallon tank on my Valkyrie. Then I was off. I had never ridden my Valkyrie with a full load before, but its 105 horsepower engine didn't even notice the extra weight. In addition, by distributing the supplies so most of the weight was low on the bike, there was almost no change in its handling characteristics. It still accelerated and handled like a sports bike. This meant that during the next several weeks I would have fun putting it through its paces, searching for my limits, and exercising my passion for riding on the edge.

When I passed through Eagle River, a town 12 miles from Anchorage, the misty rain became a cloudburst. Closely packed pea-sized water drops pelted the windshield on my motorcycle and the visor on my helmet. The downpour limited visibility. Cars and trucks traveling down the road melted into wavy patches of color as I peered through blobs of rain that were furiously attacking my windshield like a swarm of angry bees, and as oncoming traffic passed, a fine spray of water from behind the vehicle would completely blind me for a brief moment. An obstacle? As with any perceived obstacle, you can use it as an excuse to quit, or you can use it as a learning tool, something to quickly conquer, an occasion to hurl yourself forward so you can move past it and get on to whatever is next.

This was a great opportunity to learn a new skill—riding in a heavy rain. I reduced my speed, watched traffic coming from behind, and drove defensively as cars with windshield wipers swatting at rain-splashed windows bulleted along the highway.

Fortunately, within twenty minutes the rain had stopped. As I rode over the hills and descended into the Matanuska Valley, I saw long rows of gray cylindrical clouds stretching across the sky. The rows of rolled clouds were separated by narrow slits of blue sky and floated above endless fields. Silver slivers of sunlight pierced the edge of each cloud draping curtains of light from the sky to the valley below. The luminous veils signaled that I was now on the edge of the storm. In a matter of only a few minutes, the world had turned from dark, rippled, soggy, and threatening to light, clear, picturesque and promising.

After a slow 115 miles, I stopped for gas at Trapper Creek. While at the pump, a rider on a Harley Davidson motorcycle coming from the opposite direction pulled in for gas. We chatted as gas gurgled into our tanks. He said there were scattered clouds ahead, but the roads were dry, and he had not seen any rain. He was heading to Anchorage and I let him know that it had been raining in and around town and there was a good chance he would get wet.

Based on the information from a fellow biker, I decided to take my rain gear off and pack it in my saddlebag. It would be much nicer riding without the bulk. I paid for the gas and was on the road again. My Valkyrie loved the dry payment, and as it sprinted down the straightaways and leaned deeply through the curves, my spirits brightened.

I was riding on an asphalt ribbon that embellished a sparse countryside and connected an occasional cabin, with a hap-hazardly placed gas station, a rustic log lodge, and infrequent towns. Many towns had populations that could be mistaken for the age of one of its younger residents. It was only now, as I rode through the expansive Alaskan wilderness, that the full impact of what I was doing came into focus. I started thinking, "What am I doing out here in the middle of nowhere—by myself?"

In all honesty, I had many concerns before beginning this trip. During the time I spent preparing for this journey, some people freely shared their thoughts of doom with me. The many well-intentioned advisers included parents, family (excluding my wife and children who were always supportive), friends, and casual acquaintances. In some conversations, the many by-standers painted pictures in my mind about the possible dark side of this trip.

"You aren't going alone are you?"

"There are bad people in the world, so be careful."

"What will happen to you if you break down in the middle of nowhere?"

"What if you get sick?"

"Be careful of all the bears."

"Don't talk to strangers."

"You aren't driving a motorcycle down that road are you?"

"If you run off the road and get injured, you might never be found."

The wide open spaces in Alaska and western Canada meant I spent most of my time isolated from civilization, and this isolation provided fertile ground for the thoughts that were planted in my mind, a condition where people's views could all too easily become stumbling blocks. The trick, as always, is to look into the face of others' fears, to attempt to see the fears their minds harbor, to determine if for your situation the fears have flesh or if they are ghosts without substance, to include in your plans ways to avoid or mitigate dangers that might exist, and then to boldly move forward. I prepared for the things I could influence; everything else was just random events that could happen to anybody, anywhere, so it was unproductive to consider them further. What I found as I traveled was that hour-by-hour the fears faded away. The unknowns, and the fears associated with uncertainty, were far worse than the realities encountered. It is as though the force of action permeates the fears of inaction, and destroys them.

Passionate action transforms the proverbial cliff we fear plunging over in the future, into a small step in the present, and an inconsequential ripple in the path behind us. Passionate action is not about throwing all caution to the wind and being careless or reckless. It is about preparing for the road you choose to travel, then taking it as it comes, and acting based on what you find. Do not assume something will happen in the future before anything actually happens. Fears have some value, but only in the preparation. They are worthless while in action and can distract you from your goal.

For a couple of hours I had been riding, thinking, and soaking in the scenery when suddenly I rounded a corner and found myself in the middle of a bridge crossing Hurricane Gulch. It was breathtaking. I stopped to do a little exploring. The narrow steel arch bridge spanned 550 feet and the center was 260 feet above Hurricane Creek.

I climbed down the dirt bank along one side of the bridge and was surprised how steeply it dropped into the gulch. I could reach the bottom in two steps; of course, between each step I would be plummeting over 100 feet downward. Two large steel arches spanned the underside of the bridge. A series of steel beams connected the bottom of the bridge with each arch. The arches, desperately clinging to the rocky cliff walls, were all that held a narrow strip of concrete suspended above a wisp of a creek below.

I climbed out from underneath and walked along one edge of the bridge while enjoying a wonderful panoramic view. It was a narrow two-lane bridge with no pedestrian walkway. On each side were waist high metal crash rails. In the middle of the bridge, I leaned over the railing and looked straight down at the creek, 260 feet below, and my stomach began to flutter with that weird feeling you get when you think you are about to fall. While standing there transfixed by the experience, I heard the low throaty snorts of motorcycles approaching. I did not need to look to know there was more than one motorcycle coming down the road, and that they were Harleys. I turned towards the sound just in time to see four choppers riveted in a close diamond formation, approaching at 75 to 80 mph. One of the choppers had ape bars. The rider's hands grasped the motor-cycle handles at head level, forming a wide "V" in the air as if he was cheering at a football game. As the riders thundered past, I saw they were wearing Hells Angels motorcycle club colors. At the speed they were traveling, the whole experience lasted only a matter of seconds. I transitioned from breathtaking scenery and awesome height, to a sound, a glance, a deafening roar, thunder resonating in my chest, the sight of bikers disappearing around the curve on the other side of the gulch, and then silence. It was a symphony of sensation with a climactic finale.

A few miles further down the road, I stopped for gas at "The Igloo," a distinctive Alaskan landmark along the Parks Highway. Standing next to the gas station is a forty-foot high, giant white, inverted bowl-shaped, igloo-looking structure. It had doors on the bottom level and windows around it at three higher levels. The building was to be a hotel, but money problems prevented the completion of its interior. Its shell stands as an enigma on an otherwise barren landscape, sucking curious tourists off the highway like a vacuum.

About 140 miles further up the Parks Highway was another Alaskan landmark, Skinny Dick's Halfway Inn. Located halfway between the towns of Nenana and Fairbanks, it caters to locals, wayward wanderers, and tourists. Skinny Dick's logo, printed on shirts and other gift items, is a pair of copulating bears, also referred to as happy bears. Littering the walls and ceiling are various articles of clothing and dollar bills signed by past patrons. The decor, atmosphere, music, history, and souvenirs are as colorful as its name. An original piece of Alaskana.

I decided to spend my first night at the historic Ester Gold Camp, six miles west of Fairbanks. The Fairbanks Exploration Company built the camp in 1936. It supported a large gold dredging operation for about 20 years. Some of the buildings dated back to the early 1900's. I rented a room in one of two bunkhouses, built in the 1930's. The room had two single beds, a small wooden desk, a chair, and a sink. There was a toilet and shower shared with the room next door. The bathroom doors that opened into each room had two locks on them, one locked from the room side, the other locked from the bathroom side of the door. When you went into the bathroom, you locked the door leading to the other room from the bathroom side. When you left, you unlocked the door to the other room, closed your door, and locked it from your room side. I wondered if occupants from the two adjoining rooms had ever entered the bathroom at the same time, or if one occupant had ever forgot to unlock the door that opened to the other room (visions of frantic pounding on the door in the middle of the night entered my mind), or if one occupant ever forgot to lock the other door and was surprised while on the toilet or in the shower. All this was part of the rustic Wild West atmosphere, and there was no extra charge.

By the time I had unpacked my Valkyrie and settled in at the bunkhouse, I realized it was evening, I had not eaten lunch, and I was famished. I took a couple of minutes to knock the dust off myself and headed over to the hotel. A two-story hotel was located next to the bunkhouses. It was the largest building on the site. While I was going toward the dining hall in the hotel, the cook walked out onto the porch, rang a large iron triangle, and sang out, "Dinner is served." Whoa. The cook had great timing.

The hotel entrance had a large porch, partially enclosed by a white wood latticework. Tables arranged around the porch allowed diners to sit outside and feel the cool evening breeze while they ate. Inside the hotel was a small lobby area. On the right were stairs that lead up to guest rooms. A pay phone was on the wall next to the stairwell and simple wooden benches lined three walls. Straight ahead were swinging wooden doors that led into a huge dining hall. Upon entering the great hall, humid air dripping with time engulfed me, and I immediately decided to eat on the porch. Tables arranged around the hall would seat about two hundred people. A buffet table was set up down the center of the room with a generous variety of salads, vegetables, meats, breads, and desserts. The only people inside were a group of four adults wandering around trying to find the right table and a young couple with two small children. To my amazement, the waitress asked if I had reservations.

"No, but I'm hungry and would be happy with any of the 200 chairs that are not occupied." I said with a smile.

"It's not a problem right now" she said returning my smile, "but in 30 to 45 minutes this place will be full, and people will be waiting to be seated. Our buffet dinner draws people from Fairbanks and all the small towns in the surrounding area. Would you like the buffet or would you like to order off the menu?"

"The buffet looks great. I'll try it." I said.

"Have you eaten here before?"

"No."

"This is how it works. I will seat you, and then your waiter will take your drink order. When you return to the buffet table just leave your soiled dinnerware at the table. When you are finished, your waiter will bring the final bill. Eat as much as you want and enjoy."

"Thank you. Could I be seated out on the porch?"

"Certainly."

She showed me to a double table in a corner of the porch, smiled, and left. A waiter immediately came over, set up my table with sauces, butter, rolls, and a bucket to put bones and bits in. After ordering an Alaskan Amber beer, I headed toward the buffet table and filled my plate with salad, zucchini squash, buttered red potatoes, corn on the cob, fried chicken, and pasta. It was country cooking, set up like a spontaneous backcountry neighborhood potluck, with an endless variety of dishes to try. I decided not to overload my plate so I could indulge in some of the other tempting entrees when I went back for seconds.

After a leisurely and much needed dinner, I went across the road to the legendary Malemute saloon, stepped through the swinging saloon doors, and sank into a layer of sawdust and peanut shells that luxuriously covered the floor. The odor screamed old time saloon. Musky wood and peanut shell smells blended with perfume of finger foods and beer. Memorabilia from the gold rush days lined the walls. The place oozed with history. I moseyed over to the bar and immediately lost about seven decades of time. The bartender, dressed in 30's-style clothes said there was going to be a show in a little while that featured honky-tonk music, skits of the gold rush days, and poetry by Robert

Service. I secured a front row table, another Alaskan Amber, a bag of peanuts, and sat back for the rest of the evening, adding peanut shells to the floor, and soaking in the atmosphere of by-gone days. The show was over at 9:00 p.m., and I moseyed back over to the bunkhouse, fell onto the bed, and faded dead away. A phenomenal first day.

* * * * *

I was there; I had passed through the threshold of my dream. This motorcycle adventure became a reality because I took a public stand that I intended to do it (there were no other options), I confidently moved into action, and I began the process of living the dream. Public stand, confident action, and living the dream are important elements in the language of success.

As I stepped toward my dream, there were boulders in the road, wonderings down blind allies, wrong turns taken, and fears. All those situations seemed important at the time, but when looking back from the vantage point of success they became insignificant events that did not actually matter. It is interesting to look back and see how seemingly major obstacles that can distract you and force you off the path, become tomorrow's trivial circumstances.

Problems clutter any path you take, so why not go down the path that leads toward your dream? When I journey down either a physical or a mental road, I find the curves and the challenges to be the dessert of life. These are the things to seek, not to avoid. This is the correct perspective. However, success is not just going through a curve (anyone can do that); it is going through the curve as fast as possible.

Nearly everyone would like to be able to ride a motorcycle fast through the curves in a road, just for the excitement, just for the feeling of being completely alive, just to know they have the skills required to touch the edge. However, riders often have an exhaustive list of reasons for why they do not challenge themselves. This list usually contains fears such as running too wide, leaning over too far, lacking knowledge of the turn, losing traction, and traffic. No matter how long you make the list, all the fears have the same source—a lack of self-confidence. If you want to ride through the curves on the edge, you have to suck it in, take a stand, and decide that success is the only option.

The magic of taking a public stand on living your dream, focusing on succeeding, and making the decision to "just do it," is that it releases you from having to spend enormous amounts of energy avoiding the things you fear, and it allows you to concentrate on just one thing—success. Trying to prevent 5, 10, or 15 undesirable situations that might happen, requires a lot more effort than focusing on making just one thing happen. In any given situation only one thing does happen, therefore, spending energy on all your fears wastes time and energy that could be directed toward being successful at what you want to achieve.

Yes, you should consider your fears, but after that, extract the power your fears offer, then discard the fears, and avoid turning them into a project that distracts you from your main objective. Let us look at this concept relative to the case of riding a motorcycle fast along a meandering road, and in light of one possible fear—losing traction.

Here is how people make a project out of losing traction.

You evaluate your fear of losing traction and then define all the things you can do to improve the traction characteristics of your motorcycle, like tuning the suspension system for a sure grip, installing tires with a composition and tread design to maximize traction, and improving the brakes for reliable speed control when setting up for a curve. Such a course of action is seductive and may at first glance seem like a perfectly logical course of action. However, what is really happening?

- You are spending a lot of time optimizing the bike for one set of conditions. When the conditions change, the motorcycle systems are no longer optimized.

- When you finish optimizing the bike, chances are you will not be able to tell the difference between the optimized system and the one you started with. The design of a production motorcycle allows it to perform well over a broad range of conditions. Unless you are a professional motorcycle rider, and you are optimizing your bike for a specific course like a grand prix, trials competition, or a motocross race, the original design will be difficult to improve on.

- You feel good because you are busy, so you think things are going well, but this is deceptive because you are not making progress toward your goal. You are expending a considerable amount of energy on something other than your main objective of being able to ride fast through a series of curves.

- You have lost focus on the true objective and this can lead to other distractions that are not productive relative to your goal.

- You have not yet even started to address the real issue—your fear of losing traction and possibly falling.

Notice that none of the activities mentioned (tuning suspension, installing tires, improving brakes) are even about riding a motorcycle. Now let us examine how to both extract power from a fear and maintain momentum toward your goal of being able to ride on the edge, again using the fear of losing traction example.

- Determine the source of your fear. In this case, the source of the fear is falling as a result of losing traction. If you knew you would never fall, losing traction would not bother you. The truth is that even when riding conservatively you could fall off your motorcycle at any time due to a blowout, gravel on the road, or a road hazard encountered in a blind corner.

- Address your fear directly by wearing protective equipment (helmet, gloves, boots, and leathers). Tuning suspension, installing tires, and improving brakes misses the point, and does not improve your situation if you fall.

- Examine the positive side of your fear, losing traction, and see how it can help you learn to ride on the edge. By considering the dynamics of losing traction, you discover that it is really your friend. When you lose traction, the motorcycle is self-correcting a problem caused by trying to turn too sharply. When the rear tire slides, it aligns you with the direction you want to travel. In addition, when you do lose traction, you know you are riding on the edge.

- Riding instead of tuning, installing, and improving equipment is allowing you to perfect the skills that are useful relative to maintaining traction. While you are riding, you are also advancing toward your goal of being able to ride fast through a curve—to ride on the edge.

Once you have committed to pushing the limit of the man-road-machine interface, to facing and extracting power from your fears, to reaching for the edge, you must next define how progress toward your goal is measured. Speed, steering, body position and lean angle are all indicators of how you are doing at any specific moment in time. Markers in the future, however, are required to direct energy and actions toward your specific goal of riding fast along a twisting country road. When approaching a curve, you must visualize the path you wish to take from the future, decide the path through the curve, define the turn point, and then identify where you need to start breaking. Your path defines your future tactics. Your future tactics define your present actions. Knowing your present actions gives you power to move through each curve with a minimum of effort. A minimum of effort allows you to examine the results of your actions, and knowing your results allows you to improve your tactics as you set up for the next curve. Power is in the action.

Measures of how you are doing allow you to assess how to improve your performance in the next turn. Having too few measures is not helpful and having too many is a distraction. Just knowing that you were successful, or unsuccessful, in achieving your objective of going through the curve at your limit does not allow you to improve in the next curve. Without metrics, improving becomes a trial and error process. With metrics, improving is an integral part of how you do things.

If your lean angle was small when going through the last curve, then you were being too conservative. To improve, you need to consider such things as the point you start breaking, your speed, and the point you begin to turn. Braking later, increasing your speed into the curve, and beginning your turn later are all factors that will result in increased speed through the curve and thus increase the lean angle. Making adjustments and observing results for each situation you encounter will bring you closer to your goal of a high performance turn, of riding on the edge.

If your pegs were scrapping the asphalt, and you felt your back tire slip slightly, then you achieved your goal, you were on the edge. However, you still need to analyze what you did so you can apply what you learned to the next curve. You need to look at how you could have done better, because you can always improve your performance. If you stop looking for ways to improve you will get lost in the dust of those who do.

If you know you can improve, then you can. The limit to achieving the results you desire is what you say you can produce or accomplish. Nothing else. You define your limits.

*   *   *   *   *

DAY 2

I woke up, looked at my clock, and it was 2:00 a.m. The excitement of the first day on the road, the fresh air, and the nostalgic stay in a real gold mining town energized my body and mind. I dashed through desperately needed sleep to an awakening that was ready for more fresh air, more riding, more scenery, and more discoveries. However, it was 2:00 a.m., so I tried to push these thoughts out of my mind. I tossed and turned and watched every minute go by until 4:00 a.m. As it was still too early, or so I told myself, I continued to torture myself until 5:00 a.m., then decided, or more precisely my body decided, that an early start was a great idea. I got up and showered in the joint bathroom, all the time wondering if the people next door thought I was crazy. Then I packed my Valkyrie, road over to the office, drank a cup of coffee while I paid my bill, and was gone by 6:15 a.m.

It was great to be on the road again. In a few minutes, I was passing through the outskirts of Fairbanks and, at this hour, I was nearly alone on the road. The early morning air was laden with a variety of fragrances—dew dampened dirt, cut grass, spruce, and the perfume of crisp, clean, clear air, untainted by the mechanized industry that would later spoil the sweet aroma of this moment. Early morning sunlight bathing the grassy, bushy, dew-soaked world created a dazzling shimmer that contrasted sharply with the black leather coat and pants I was wearing. The effect was strange because I felt completely integrated into the world and completely separate from it at the same instant. A shadow. A glistening sunlit world and black leather. A part, but distinctly apart.

About thirty miles outside Fairbanks I passed a six-foot tall Alaskan mosquito. People who read stories about the large mosquitoes in Alaska usually think the tales are exaggerated, so I stopped and took pictures so I could show folks what we contend with up here. Actually, the mosquito, ingeniously constructed from burl wood, stood lounging in the morning sun outside the Knotty Shop. I would have liked to go inside and look around, but the shop did not open for two hours.

I continued southeast out of Fairbanks along the Richardson Highway for ninety miles, then stopped for gas at Delta Junction. This is the official northern terminus of the Alaska Highway. From Delta Junction to its southern terminus in Dawson

Creek the road was 1422 miles long when constructed in 1942. Road improvement projects over the years have straightened the Al-Can (what many people call the Alaska Highway), decreasing the physical distance by 32 miles. The Canadian government is continually improving the Al-Can and, compared with the bog-infested road of 1942, the current road is a reliable motorway. However, roadwork can stretch for several miles, conditions along these sections can be challenging, and just off the highway the country the Al-Can passes through is still rugged, remote, and unforgiving.

After leaving Delta Junction, I was riding through a high country valley with unique and varied scenery. Long stretches of road were flat and straight (especially outside Tok).

Along one stretch, a narrow shoulderless road sliced through a large open meadow filled with fireweed in full bloom. A gentle breeze made waves in the pinkish purple floral sea that stretched out before me and faded into the horizon. In the background were snow-capped peaks of the Wrangell Mountains. Riding a motorcycle through a cartoon-colored sea laid down beneath florescent white mountains made this a surrealistic scene. The scene was real, but had a dreamlike quality. I hovered above the floral sea, absorbed and fascinated by the illusion. A combination of perspective and my current speed made it seem as though I was motionless. Then, with a twist of the wrist, I began to float through the pastel ocean.

Along another section of road was a black spruce forest. Black spruce trees found in marshy soil, in northern climates, have a very slow growth rate (particularly if they are on top of a discontinuous band of permafrost, which is common in this area). A tree six feet tall may be decades or even centuries old. In addition, building stable roads in the marshy terrain found in this area required that they are elevated several feet by a bed of rock and gravel.

The black spruce forest I was riding through on the raised road was a forest in every sense of the word. The tree stand was dense and sprinkled with shrubs and grasses. The interesting thing was that as far as I could see, all the trees in this particular forest were only 5 to 10 feet tall, and the shrubs and grasses were also smaller, putting the entire miniature forest into perfect proportions. Since the only frame of reference for size was the trees in the forest, and they were all miniatures, riding along this elevated section of road created an illusion of being a giant, on a giant motorcycle, looking down upon a great forest. Another cartoon-like scene.

For me, traveling on a motorcycle maximizes the pleasure of a trip. When on a motorcycle you are in the scenery and a part of the world. When taking a trip enclosed in a car, scenery is something out there you sporadically notice between the barrage of music, conversation, snacks, coffee, and boredom. I do not mean to imply that one way of traveling is better than another, just noting that they are significantly different. Different in ways that words cannot communicate. A huge chasm in understanding exists between people who have experienced the difference between traveling by car and traveling by motorcycle, and those who have not had both experiences. If you have never scuba dived, or sky dived, or parasailed, or ridden in a hot air balloon, you cannot understand those experiences or have them transferred to you through words alone. If you think that because you have been swimming you can understand what scuba diving is like, you are wrong. They are two completely different worlds, connected only by the similarity that both activities involve water.

*   *   *   *   *

The fact that you can only know by doing is as true of riding a motorcycle as it is of living a dream, or succeeding in achieving an aspiration. People can describe what they have experienced, they can give advice, but do not let others words replace the experience, or dissuade you from passionate action. Take a public stand for living your dream. Enter into the arena. Be a participant in your virtuous dreams. If you wish to understand, to live your dream, to close the chasm of understanding that exists between being a spectator and being a participant, you must have the experience. As you are moving toward your dream, keep the chasm in mind, and gain understanding through your action, not through projections made from others words.

*   *   *   *   *

Near mid-afternoon, as I approached the Alaskan-Canadian border, I began to hear an occasional rattle coming from my motorcycle. The road was intermittent asphalt and gravel, and I would hear the rattle only on the roughest parts of the road. The noise was subtle, and I wondered if maybe the sound had always been there but I had not noticed it before. I stopped for gas at the Border City Lodge, three and a half miles north of Canada.

After gassing up, I examined my entire bike but was unable to find the source of the sound. The kickstand on the motorcycle was spring-loaded and I thought that perhaps this was rattling when I hit a bump.

The road between the Border City Lodge and the US customs had long rough sections; as I rode the rattling sound became louder and more frequent. I pulled over in a parking area just before the US customs building to take another look. This time the problem was easy to spot. The bracket that attaches the right rear foot peg and the muffler to the frame had two bolts that were about to drop out. My tools were located under the motorcycle seat. The sun was scorching hot, so rather than break my bike apart for tools in my leathers with no shade around, I just hand-tightened the bolts. Canadian customs was only 17 miles to the south of the US customs office (at this border crossing there are two different stations separated by 17 miles, northbound traffic only stops at US customs and southbound traffic only stops at the Canadian customs office). If I could not find any shade around the Canadian customs office for working on my bike, I would torque the bolts at Beaver Creek, where I was planning to spend the night. Halfway to Canadian customs, I had to stop again and hand-tighten the bolts.

When I got to the Canadian customs checkpoint, there were only three cars in front of me so I did not have to wait in the heat for long. When I was in motion I could unzip all six vents in my leather jacket and the circulating air would keep me cool. But when I stopped, my black leathers soaked up the sun and soon the heat began to poach my sweat-bathed body. Before long, the car in front of me drove through customs into Canada and

I pulled up to the checkpoint. A border guard at the window asked me to turn my motorcycle off and remove my helmet (she wanted a good look at my face).

"Where are you headed?" she asked.

"To visit my parents in Washington State," I replied.

"How long are you going to be there?"

"About a week, then I'll be returning to Anchorage."

"Are you going to the motorcycle rally?"

"No. I'm not aware of any motorcycle rallies."

"Oh. Earlier, there were a couple of bikers going to a motorcycle rally, but I think they were riding BMW's. Are you carrying any alcohol or cigarettes?"

"No."

"Do you have any pepper spray?"

"No."

"Do you have any guns or weapons of any kind?"

"No, just a knife."

"What kind of knife?"

"A buck knife here on my belt."

"Let me see." I pulled it out and showed it to her. "O.K. You can go on through. Enjoy your trip."

Just past the checkpoint were three large shaded parking areas with tables and benches where the border guards do vehicle searches. They were all empty.

"I have a couple of bolts loose and was wondering if I could pull into one of your stalls and tighten them," I said.

She looked up at me with a deadly serious face and said, "don't ever tell an immigrations officer you have a bolt loose."

A moment of silence, a smile, then a returned smile. A bad

joke but you never try to irritate a gun-toting immigrations officer and she did let me use one of the shaded stalls.

I checked the torque on all the bolts on the motorcycle. The only ones loose were the two that had nearly fallen out, and two others on the same bracket on the opposite side of the bike. Before leaving Anchorage, I had new tires mounted, and it appeared as though the mechanic did not properly torque these bolts when reinstalling the wheel.

By the time I had finished and put all my tools away, the other two stalls had vehicles parked in them and the border guards were searching the vehicles. In both cases the travelers seemed to be obvious candidates for detainment (although I thought I might fit the profile as well—a motorcycle rider, black leather jacket, black leather pants, black leather gloves, a knife in a black leather case on my black leather belt, and I hadn't shaved for several days, but I guess I have an honest face). The vehicle parked in one stall was an old VW van with four middle-aged adults who looked like hippies. Wow! It had been a couple of decades since I'd observed that scene. The other vehicle, a truck, had two gang wanna-be's in it. Thankfully, I was ready to leave. It looked like things were starting to get busy at Canadian customs.

I stopped for the evening at Beaver Creek just past the border, mainly because it was not one of the main towns in the Yukon Territories and I thought it would be interesting to see what a small isolated Canadian town was like. After checking into a hotel, I went outside, walked around the sparse town, and ended up in the visitors' center. The town promoted many activities around Beaver Creek including nature walks, hikes, and flight-seeing trips. All the activities took more than the hour or two

I had to kill before dinner, so I spent some time talking to the attendant about the colorful history of this border town. It surprised me to find out that Beaver Creek is a major stop for tour buses traveling the Al-Can. I learned that Beaver Creek only had about 40 permanent residents, but during the summer the population swelled to around 300 to handle the tourists. Sure enough, as the dinner hour neared, tour buses converged from the north and the south and began to assemble at various places along the highway that cut through Beaver Creek. So much for my idea of staying in a small, unspoiled town.

The main event each evening was a barbecue and a North Country melodrama complete with honky-tonk music. I decided to go and see what attracted folks from around the world to this town. The barbeque was in a large building. A center stage formed a hub and long rows of tables covered with red and white checkered tablecloths were arranged like wheel spokes that radiated from the stage area.

The food was O.K., but it seemed to be more of a barbeque-like meal, which consisted of a variety of meats served with a salad, baked potato, and beans. The entertainment was probably O.K. too. However, all the people who attended seemed so plastic to me. Herds of people stampeded from the buses into the hotels, then from the hotels to the evening entertainment. They ate, then chewed their cud, and mooed contently. Before the dinner show even started, the people near me were already talking about being herded into buses the next morning, herded into several predetermined tourist traps along the highway, then being rounded up and funneled into another show about life in the great North Country. Of course, they did not use the term 'herded', but the words used did not hide what was happening.

Most tour groups provide high quality adventures and I love to see vacationers enjoy the wonders of this unspoiled land. However, in this case the tour guides I met were from places like New York and Chicago. No wonder the tour these people were on was so superficial. Plastic people produce plastic experiences.

I hope never to trade in my spontaneity, my imagination, or my thirst for adventure for a nose ring and a leash. If I do end up wearing a nose ring, I hope someone will show mercy, abduct me from the travel cult, take me to a deprogramming center, and rekindle my passion for adventure before mediocrity smothers my spirit. I found the whole experience to be very depressing and vowed to avoid crowds during the rest of my trip.

DAY 3

Only 5 hours of sleep again. This trip was like a breath of spring air, energizing and revitalizing my body, my mind, and my spirit. I woke up at 2:30 a.m. and churned the covers on my bed until 5:30 a.m. Trying to sleep was futile so I laced, snapped and zipped my leathers on and then packed my motorcycle, drank a cup of coffee, and was cruising down the road by 6:00 a.m.

As I traveled south from Beaver Creek, the roads became progressively worse. First rough in spots, then rough in stretches, and finally rough in three to five km sections with loose gravel and rocks. In places, the brush came right to the edge of the road. Limited visibility to the right, to the left, and around corners made being alert imperative. This was desolate country. Along these sections of brush-choked Yukon roads, it was possible that an animal such as a bear, caribou, moose, sheep, porcu-pine, or beaver might wish to use the road at the same time and same place as me. A collision with even a small animal when traveling on a motorcycle, in a remote area, could be disastrous. The condition of the road remained poor for over 100 miles before changing back to having only occasional problem spots.

I stopped at a wilderness viewing area 70 miles south of Beaver Creek where there was a clear view of the Donjek River valley. The sprawling valley provided a sharp contrast to the Ice Field Ranges in the background, a part of the St. Elias Mountains. One of the peaks in this mountain range is Canada's tallest mountain, Mt. Logan, which is 19,850 feet high. The Ice Field Ranges are eighty-five percent covered in ice and have some of the largest, non-polar ice fields in North America. At their heart, the ice fields are up to 200 feet thick.

The next town I passed through was Burwash Landing. This town was established in 1904 as a trading post during a gold rush in this area.

Nearby was the town of Destruction Bay. Destruction Bay had its beginnings as a camp during the construction of the Al-Can. It got its name when it was destroyed during a windstorm in 1942.

Beyond Destruction Bay, the road wove its way along the western shore of Kluane Lake. Kluane is a corruption of the Southern Tutchone Indian name for "lake of the big fish". The lake, with a surface area of 150 square miles, is the largest body of water in the Yukon Territory.

I pulled off the road and onto a gravel bar next to the lake. The spot was rich in contrasts. Behind me were sheer mud-brown cliffs. Cut into the rocky cliff was a narrow gorge where No Name creek roared and churned into the still lake. A coarse gray gravel beach lined the lake. Along the shoreline was an enormous piece of driftwood, a ten-foot long section of tree; the trunk was three-feet in diameter, with a contorted root system at its base. The tree was bleached white by the sun and worn smooth from water and sand action. This huge piece of driftwood, tossed upon the dry gravel beach during the thunderous fury of a storm, stood as a lone sculpture on an otherwise barren shoreline (dramatic storms are common in this are). The lake itself was tranquil and a beautiful deep turquoise green. On the far shore, the lake butted up against an expansive green-forested valley. To the right and to the left the lake extended toward the horizon, stopped in its expansion by abrupt walls of distant mountains. At this spot, on this gravel bar, in all directions, serenity and severity clashed like a symphony of drums and violins.

I remounted my motorcycle and continued toward the southern toe of the lake. There was a faint hint along the opposite shoreline of what appeared to be mist or smoke. While crossing the bridge over the Slims River flats, I discovered the haze was the result of the wind picking up glacial silt, which has a consistency of flour, and carrying it out over the lake. A "Danger High Winds" sign just before the bridge made it clear that this was a usual condition.

After crossing the bridge, the road skirted the edge of the lake for a while then turned east into a valley. At Historic Milepost 1053, a gravel road led to the ruins of Silver City, once a stopping point on the wagon road between Whitehorse and the placer gold fields of Kluane Lake. I decided to take the three-mile side trip to see what Silver City looked like. What I found was unexpected. There were several log structures built in the early 1900's (ca 1904 to 1915), which were still in fair shape. The town's layout was clear and consisted of a roadhouse, trading post, and barracks for the Northwest Mounted Police. Some of the buildings were still intact, others had a section of roof that had collapsed (likely due to years of neglect and a heavy snow load during the winter). This is the first time I had been in a real ghost town that was not a tourist trap. I was alone in a desolate, forested, empty settlement. It was fun to wander, explore, and fantasize about the past, and there was a tingle of excitement about the possibility of bears also wandering around, curious about the ruins. A wonderful side trip that was well worth the time.

I did not see any bears at Silver City; in fact, I had not yet seen any bears. This was about to change. Outside of Haines Junction, the road became narrow with trees and brush along the sides. As I was riding, a black bear walked from the right side onto the road in front of me, stopped in the middle, paused briefly to look at me coming towards it, and then walked off the road to the left. I was excited about t g a photograph of a bear—up close. I slowed when I was alongside it. The bear was a huge male. He was walking along the side of the road in the same direction I was traveling. His mouth was hanging open and he was panting like he had been running. The bear made eye contact with me, and his expression was a very plain "don't give me any crap" look as he walked rapidly along the side of the road. Because the bear appeared to be upset about something,

I decided not to stop and take pictures. However, the memory was burned into my brain.

At Historic Milepost 996 is a replica of the Canyon Creek Bridge, built in 1904 by roadhouse keepers Gilbert Skelly and Sam McGee (the same person that was made famous by Robert Service's ballad "The Cremation of Sam McGee"). This was an important link for travelers along the wagon road between Whitehorse and Silver City. Crews rebuilt the bridge during construction of the Alaska Highway in 1942, and then abandoned it the following year after rerouting the highway. The Yukon Government restored the bridge in 1987.

Under a central section of the bridge, rough-hewn logs were interlocked like the walls of a small box-shaped log cabin forming a mid-span support. Two smooth parallel wheel paths were made by placing wooden planks over the log surface of the bridge. It was interesting to see the ingenious methods used to build log bridges during that period.

On the outskirts of Whitehorse I was surprised to see a large buffalo grazing beside the road. I later learned there was once a large buffalo herd that roamed this area of the Yukon. These are magnificent animals and it was exciting to see one roaming free.

Upon my arrival in Whitehorse, I found a place to stay at the Hawkins House Bed and Breakfast, a Victorian house located near the city center. The white house had blue and mauve accents around the windows, roof, porch, and balconies. Inside, the floors were finished in a light maple wood. The foyer had a bench next to the door where you could sit and take off your shoes (a custom in the north). There was a throw rug at one end of the bench to leave your shoes on before entering the main part of the house. The guest rooms were all upstairs. A large door at the end of the hall led into the kitchen and living area of the main house. This door was closed and locked during the evening hours so only the guest rooms were accessible through the front door of the Victorian home. I stayed in a pleasant room filled with native art and French doors that opened onto a small balcony overlooking the street in front of the house.

When I checked in, the host said that breakfast started at 8:00 a.m. I smiled politely and indicated I would likely be on the road by 6:00 a.m. so they should not plan on me being at breakfast.

"Where are you headed?" the host asked.

"I'm going to Dawson City, spending one night there, and then heading down the Alaska Highway to Watson Lake where I'll take the Cassiar Highway to Washington state."

"The Cassiar Highway?"

"Yes."

"I've been down the Cassiar and would recommend you avoid that road at all costs. It's in terrible condition. You should take the Alaskan Highway all the way to Washington," she said.

"I'm planning to take the Alaskan Highway on the return trip and wanted some different scenery on the way down."

"I would not recommend the Cassiar, but I suppose you know what you are doing," she said. However, the tone in her voice suggested that she did not really believe I knew what I was doing at all.

The curious glances I got from the neighbors as I was unloading my Valkyrie in front of this Victorian house, dressed in full leathers, unshaven, and hair matted and tangled like old moss on the side of a tree, gave me the feeling that I was not a common sight. My impression was that they did not get many bikers staying here. However, I am sure the locals enjoy the variety of clientele that comes and goes at the Hawkins House B&B. Once I changed clothes and cleaned up, I was reasonably presentable—and when I went outside, I seemed to fade back into humanity.

Yesterday at the barbecue in Beaver Creek, I had learned from one of the cattle-like tourists that there was a fire near Fox Lake between Whitehorse and Dawson City. The fire had jumped the road on July 3, causing power outages and closing the highway along that stretch of road. On July 4, a pilot car escorting vehicles through the burn area had to turn back because of dangerous conditions. I was planning to ride to Dawson City tomorrow (July 6), so I walked to the Whitehorse Visitor Center to get an update on the status of the fire. The woman at the information desk said the road had been open most of that day, but there were delays because they were requiring pilot cars to take groups through the burn area. She also mentioned that at times flare-ups would close the road for several hours during the day. The best times to travel were early in the morning or late in the afternoon because that was when the winds in that area were calmest.

I was going to try to get through the fire zone tomorrow. My plans were to take a two-day side trip from Whitehorse to Dawson City and back to Whitehorse. Because of the fire, I decided to have an alternate plan. If I could not get past the fire at Fox Lake, I would go to Skagway instead of Dawson City. If

I made it through to Dawson City, I just hoped I could get back without any problems the following day. If there were a delay on the return, then I would just deal with it. The excitement of an unexpected and random event, such as a fire, potentially affecting my plans added spice to the trip. It did not discourage, it created texture that intensified the experience.

* * * * *

Fear of the unknown can have a paralyzing affect on people. To succeed in your endeavors it is important to understand this beast. Fear helps you to survive by making you cautious in unfamiliar situations. Fear also helps you identify possible dangers, allowing you to take actions to minimize adverse impacts that may be associated with unfamiliar situations. What you must remember is the possible dangers do not actually exist. Danger is only a short make-believe story you tell yourself that is characterized by a linkage to a fear. Some examples follow.

"If I do poorly on this presentation, I will be fired."

"If I ride too fast down this winding road, I will be killed."

"If I try to water ski, I will fall."

"If I start a new business, I will lose all our savings."

"If I try to dance, I will look like an idiot."

"If I ask for a raise, I will be rejected."

"If I am trapped behind the fire, it will ruin my motorcycle trip."

Danger is an assessment you make from a situation or set of facts that is triggered by fear of a future action. It is an extrapolation but not a reality, and usually it is not even a result

from the action. For example, in the above comments we can
. identify the fear and the associated danger (which assumes only
one outcome).

- poor presentation = fired
- ride fast = killed
- try to water ski = fall
- start new business = lose money
- dance = look like an idiot
- ask = rejected
- trapped = bad trip

The indicated dangers are possible outcomes but not necessarily the outcome from the action. Each of these fears are only
one of hundreds of possible outcomes (if you ask for a raise you
might get it, you might be told you are already being considered for a raise, you might be given some advice for improving
your performance so you will be eligible for a raise in the future).
The danger story you tell yourself helps you avoid extrapolated
events that you believe may lead to an undesirable consequence.
In that way, fear can be your friend, but the danger born from
your fear is still just a fantasy, a mental creation, and a fabrica-
tion. If you knew the outcome of your actions, it would mean
you could tell the future. That is nonsense. If something you
fear does not happen (most likely the case), it is not danger, it
is nothing. If something you fear does happen, it is not danger either, it is a learning experience that will make you better,
stronger, more resilient (falling is a part of learning to water ski
and everyone who has learned to water ski has improved themselves by falling—each fall teaches you what not to do next time
you try). It is best just to acknowledge a danger as one of many

outcomes, act to mitigate any adverse concerns you may have, and go forward. It is debilitating to live life as if the danger will happen, as if the danger is real, letting the fear it nurtures paralyze you, freeze you, and keep you from being in action. This is when fear is not a friend—it is an enemy.

It is worthwhile to examine how you use fear in your life, during situations where you are successful. When I am riding my motorcycle on a winding, tree-lined road, I look as far as possible into the turn in front of me, and adjust my speed so I can safely negotiate the part of the road I can see. If I notice the turn gets tighter up ahead, I adjust my path. If the turn begins to open up, I increase my speed until I can see the road straighten out, then I open the throttle and accelerate back up to the speed I was going before the curve. When I come out of the turn, I have succeeded because I stayed in action despite my fears. The stories I told myself about possible dangers (potholes, gravel, a stalled car) kept me alert to avoidance plans in case they were required. The danger did not happen because of the way I reacted to the situation. I maintained forward energy and even increased energy as it became clear the danger story I was telling myself was a fantasy. If the road obstacles did appear during the turn, then there would be no danger either, because I was anticipating appropriate avoidance measures. If you do not hit a pothole, it is not dangerous to you.

This is all very logical, but just the opposite of what often happens when we have fear or sense danger. To draw on the earlier analogy, frequently in life when you see the corner, you believe the danger is real, and you stop or go another way. In my case, the fire on the road to Dawson City and the bad condition of the

DAWSON CITY.

Yukon Hotel.

Boiler where Sam McGee was cremated.

Diamond Tooth Gertie's gambling hall.

Boardwalk sidewalk.

Author Robert Service's cabin.

DAWSON CITY TO WHITEHORSE.

Beaver dam on a branch of the Klondike River.

Leaving Dawson City.

Field of fireweed.

DAWSON CITY TO WHITEHORSE.

Fire along road.

Fire flare-up north of Fox Lake.

Burned area in the middle of Fox Lake fire.

Fire looking from the south end of Fox Lake.

WHITEHORSE TO WATSON LAKE.

Jake's Corner – 1920's truck with owner,
Dave Gilbert.

Under the hood.

Riding a wild mosquito.

Swift River.

WHITEHORSE TO WATSON LAKE.

Signs showing distance to planets (placed by aliens?).

A part of the 'Sign Post Forest' at Watson Lake.

More signs.

WATSON LAKE TO ISKUT.

Mountain sheep on the road.

Clear mountain lake
16 miles down the
Cassiar Highway.

Leaving Good Hope Lake.

Waterfall
8 miles outside
Good Hope
Lake.

Tatogga Lake Resort Lodge.

Honeymoon
Cache where
I stayed the
night.

Sign on repair shop wall.

Repair
shop.

ISKUT TO QUESNEL.

My motorcycle at Maziadin Junction, day two on the Cassiar.

Glacier on Stewart-Hyder Highway.

Quesnel park.

Downtown Quesnel.

Water wheel in Quesnel.

Bridge in Quesnel.

Cassiar Highway both initially looked like significant problems, and fears could have caused my plans to change. Not going to Dawson City or traveling down the Cassiar Highway would have compromised my dream and I would have missed some unique and memorable experiences. To make your dreams come true you must have a passion for the winding roads, the little traveled paths, and the new experiences. Let the details of your dream burn like Kennedy's sending "a man to the moon by the end of this decade," and maintain the forward energy. Let your fears help you through the corner, not stop you, or change your path.

Also, like Kennedy's sending "a man to the moon by the end of this decade," by telling other people what you intend to do, by taking a public stand on a matter, you increase your intensity, your focus, your commitment. A public stand is a contract you make between you and the world, and your integrity will not allow you to break the contract. Your public commitment will carry you through difficult times, motivate you to keep trying, and help you stay in action.

* * * * *

DAY 4

Again, I woke up before my alarm went off. It was 5:00 a.m. I quietly dressed, packed my Valkyrie, and was on the road shortly after 6:00 a.m.

It is interesting to me how much energy you have when you are living a dream. At home, I needed an alarm clock so I could drag myself out of bed at 6:00 a.m. and get ready for work. On weekends I would not wake up until 8:00 or 9:00 a.m.

Even though I had no fixed schedule, and could sleep as long as I wanted during this trip, I always woke up, without an alarm clock, by 5:00 to 6:00 a.m., and was on the road by 6:00 to 7:00 a.m. It was as if I had tapped into a source of energy radiating from the core of the universe. I am convinced, living a dream energizes its fulfillment.

I rode through the deserted streets of Whitehorse, turned off the Alaska Highway (Hwy 1), and headed north on the Klondike Loop Highway (Hwy 2). This road connects Whitehorse to Dawson City (327 miles). Whitehorse is the Yukon's largest city with 20,000 people and Dawson City is the Yukon's second largest city having a population of 1,000. The Yukon Territory is larger than the states of Washington and Oregon together, but it is sparsely populated.

When I arrived at Fox Lake there was an orange Yukon Territorial truck parked facing me in the northbound lane, with two stop signs positioned on each edge of the lane. The fact that I was the only one at the checkpoint raised a concern that the road might be closed. I parked my Valkyrie in the middle of the lane and went over to talk with the ranger. She said the road was open but the pilot car would not be arriving for 15 or 20 minutes.

I was alone at the checkpoint for about five minutes, but eventually large transport trucks and RV's started to line up behind me. It was interesting to observe this because since leaving Whitehorse, I had the distinct feeling of being the only person heading north on this road, but the illusion was a result of long distances between vehicles rather than actually being alone.

While waiting for the pilot car to arrive, I chatted with the truck driver behind me. I told him I had heard mixed stories about the condition of the Cassiar Highway and asked if he had been down the road recently. He said he drove the Cassiar Highway three weeks ago and it was in good shape. He went on to say that there is some roadwork going on and that he hoped the road was never improved because it was one of the few places he knew that was still unspoiled by tourists.

"It is just bad enough to keep all but the most adventurous away," the trucker added with a smile.

The books I read before the trip had varied descriptions concerning the condition of the Cassiar Highway. Now, in the last two days, I had heard everything from "it is terrible so avoid it at all costs," to "they have been working on the road and it is in good shape." This clearly demonstrates that you cannot know something until you know it through your own experience. Secondhand information is a story that comes from people's interpretations of their experiences, and it will have different perspectives depending upon the person relating the event. The stories people tell are their views of what they experienced, but they are not the actual experiences. Conflicts in secondhand information do not mean one view is right and another view is wrong. From each individual's perspective, they have honestly described what was true for them. This is a problem with information from others. When you hear another person's view, you need to beware how you use that information. If you have a dream that sees the possibilities differently than others, do not let their views alter your course of action. Even though I had the benefit of many peoples' first-hand experience of their journey down the Cassiar Highway, I would not know what it was really like until I had experienced it for myself. I am an individual, and my view of a situation will be different from another person's view of the same situation. We all have different interests, likes, and dislikes and these differences shade how we relate our experiences to others. If you really want to know, you must have the experience, you must immerse yourself in the river of your dream.

A pilot car approached from the opposite direction, pulled over to the side of the road, and let a line of vehicles continue on their journey south. When the last car passed, the pilot car turned around and directed us to follow it north through the fire zone. I was directly behind the orange truck that led the parade of long haul trucks, cars, RV's, and one lone motorcycle.

Smoke permeated the air as we convoyed through the burn area, but the affect was not what I expected based on past experiences sitting around campfires and having smoke sting my eyes and irritate my nose. The smoke in the smoldering forest was dilute and everywhere. It did not burn my nose or make my eyes water, and the air had a sweet, corky, mossy aroma that was surprisingly pleasant.

Shortly after the pilot car left the checkpoint, I saw a rabbit run onto the road and stop in the right hand lane. There was no obvious reaction by the orange pilot truck.

"The driver surely sees the rabbit," I thought. Still no reaction.

"The rabbit surely sees the pilot truck." The rabbit had a dazed, semiconscious gaze in its eyes.

The orange pilot truck continued on a straight path down the road. As it continued to approach the rabbit, I thought the truck would swerve at anytime. No indication of a course change.

"The rabbit will surely run off the road at any second," the conversation continued in my mind.

"Rabbit," my mind shouted.

"Rabbit."

"RUN RABBIT!"

No reaction to what was happening from either the driver or the rabbit. Then, the orange pilot trucks right wheels thumped loudly as they went over the rabbit. The result was like an explosion. Bits of fur were still floating in the air as I drove past the site where the carnage occurred. I could not believe it. Poof. No more rabbit. The truck never changed course and did not swerve even after hitting the rabbit. It was a casual act. It was purposeful. They murdered the rabbit.

"Ass holes!"

The death of the rabbit seemed to accentuate the death of the forest we were driving though. Everywhere, I saw burned and smoldering trees, small fires, and flames leaping from trees like a giant flamethrower. This was the first time I had actually been in an active forest fire. It was devastating.

The devastation I saw made me want to stop and take pictures but my position directly behind the murderous orange pilot car made that problematic. I was sure the rabbit killers would not appreciate my leaving the parade, so I decided to stop tomorrow on the way back to Whitehorse. The orange pilot truck led us 20 miles down the road then pulled over just before Braeburn Lodge where it let the parade continue north on its own.

My trip plan was to stop for gas about every 60 to 80 miles. There were two reasons for this. It would give me a chance to stretch regularly so I would not get stiff. Also, the range of my motorcycle was just over twice that distance, and as there were areas where gas stations were scarce and there were times that gas stations that did exist were out of gas, I could minimize the chance of being stranded by keeping my gas tank at least half full. This turned out to be a good strategy. I had planned to get gas at Braeburn Lodge, but when I stopped, the pumps were not working. The next gas station was 50 to 60 miles up the highway. No problem, just a little texture added to the trip.

Twenty-five miles further north I stopped at the Montague Roadhouse ruins. There were two structures. A cabin with a grass-covered sod roof, still intact, and a two-story lodge without a roof. By the size of the trees growing inside the walls of the lodge, it appeared as though the roof had been missing for at least 20 or 30 years, but the walls themselves were in good shape. Inside the lodge on one side was a root cellar. I speculated that the cellar was located near where the kitchen had once been located. The Montague Roadhouse is the remains of one of 52 places, along the wagon trail between Whitehorse and Dawson City, where travelers could get food and lodging in the early 1900's.

My next stop was at Carmacks for gas. The town's namesake, George Carmack, established a trading post at this location in 1892. He was the one who subsequently found gold in Rabbit Creek (later renamed Bonanza) and its tributary Eldorado in 1986. Those finds fueled the last great Yukon gold rush.

Outside Carmacks is the Five Fingers Rapids Recreation Site along the shores of the Yukon River. Five river channels, created by four vertical pillars of erosion-resistant basalt rock, formed one of the most treacherous sections of the river for stern-wheelers that ran between White horse and Dawson City during the early 1900's. This area of the Yukon River was known to the Tutchone Indians as Tthi-cho nadezhe, meaning "rocks (standing up) in the water."

Further north, at Pelly Crossing, a Selkirk Indian community, there was an old, weathered, wooden, flat-bottomed riverboat beside the road. There were not any signs indicating anything about its age or use, which was great because then I had the opportunity to look and imagine what its past might have been. It had a large rope-grooved post at the bow of the boat, an enclosed cabin at the stern, and it looked perfect for trading and hauling supplies between ports along the river systems in this region of the Yukon.

It was a beautiful sunny morning when I left Whitehorse, but the further north I went the colder and more menacing the weather became. About 45 miles south of Dawson City it started raining, and the rain continued intermittently for periods that lasted 10 to 20 minutes—on and off, and on and off. Outside Dawson City, I had my first sight of the Klondike River and I had to stop and take a picture of my Valkyrie next to it. The name Klondike came from a Man Indian word (Thron Diuck) meaning "hammer water," describing posts hammered into the river bottom to form salmon traps. Later, after gold was found in Bonanza Creek tributary, Klondike became synonymous with wealth and adventure. As I stood along the bank, I could not help but notice that the word Klondike still dripped with adventure.

Riding into Dawson City was like going through a time warp. I rode from the modern city of Whitehorse in July of 1998, through a forest, into another city, and suddenly it was July during the turn of the 20th century. The town, a national historic site since the early 1960's, was comprised mostly of buildings from the gold rush boom days that had been restored to their original splendor. None of the streets were paved. Marshy soil and permafrost creates an unstable environment for building. Freeze-thaw cycles make the ground heave, causing buildings to shift and the streets to roll. You can see the affects of frost heaves as you are walking on the undulating boardwalk sidewalks along the storefronts. The buildings were built on stilts, and needed routine adjustments with shims to keep them level.

All the buildings were fascinating both inside and out, and it was easy to lose myself in the history of this place as I wandered the streets. I saw the boiler where Sam McGee was cremated in 1893; the sod-roofed log cabin where Robert Service wrote his famous poems like "The Shooting of Dan McGrew," "The Spell of the Yukon," "The Ballad of One-Eyed Mike," and "The Cremation of Sam McGee," and I ended up at Diamond Tooth Gerties, a gambling hall complete with honky-tonk music and a cancan floor show.

When I entered Diamond Tooth Gerties, a big man at the front door asked me to check my knife. Like an outlaw or rowdy miner in the middle of the gold rush days, I had to check my gun (knife in this case) at the door. A unique experience. I handed my knife to the man and he gave me a token to retrieve it with when I left. Across the spacious gambling hall was a large wooden stage with wooden tables and chairs strewn around in front of it. To my right was a long wooden bar with people and stools cluttering the front of it. Directly between the stage and me were slot machines, and to my left were roulette, poker, and Black Jack tables. Hanging heavily over the entire room was a roar of unintelligible words punctuated with occasional shouts of excitement and eruptions of laughter.

The first cancan show did not start for over an hour so I thought I would gamble while waiting. I started at the Black Jack table, where I bought $100.00 in chips. My strategy was to sit there, play until the show started, then cash in my chips and get all my money back. Instead, I promptly lost the entire one hundred dollars. That did not last long, so I bought $50.00 more in chips and went to the Roulette table with the idea to win all my money back and then go watch the show. Soon after arriving, I started looking around and somehow all my chips had evaporated into thin air. Wow. I was feeling low, but decided to get another $50.00 in tokens and sit around playing the slot machines. This was my absolute limit, if I lost it, I decided to just go to the bar and wait for the show. Within a few minutes, I had won over $100.00. Yes, that felt good.

When the cancan show started, I found a table near the front, and sat down to relax and watched the show. The honky-tonk piano player and the performers did a great job of getting the audience involved in the action and I fell deeper into the time warp. I was beginning to believe I was actually in the early 1900's. After the show, I went back to the slot machines and increased my winnings by $200.00. Now I was $150.00 up for the night. I decided to gamble with another $50.00 to see if I could better my earnings. I put aside a few chips as souvenirs and lost the remainder of the $50.00, so I quit for the evening, $100.00 up.

When I left Diamond Tooth Gerties, it was 10:30 p.m. However, it was only a couple weeks past summer solstice so the sun was still shining like a bright, mid-afternoon day. As I walked down the boardwalk toward the Fifth Avenue bed-and-breakfast where I was staying, I could hear load music coming from a saloon down the street. When I was about half a block away from the saloon, a young guy was suddenly and violently ejected out the door. He was followed by another much bigger guy, and then a half dozen spectators emerged. There were some heated in-your-face words exchanged between the young ejectee and the big ejector. Finally, the fellow that was ejected from the saloon threw a punch at the big burly guy. Obviously not too bright. The burly guy blocked the punch, then threw a counter punch to the side of his head, sending the young guy flying off the boardwalk sidewalk, two feet above the street, and landing on his back. Several of the spectators went down and grabbed the young guy. Everyone seemed to be shouting at someone. A few more heated words were yelled by the young guy who had just picked himself up off the ground (he had not yet learned his lesson), then he was coaxed to leave by some of the spectators and the burly guy went back into the saloon. What I had just witnessed was a bouncer evicting an unruly patron from the saloon. This completed the time warp. I was in the Wild West.

I had a wonderful time, and the entertainment, food, boardwalk brawl, and lodging in Dawson city did not cost anything. I was lucky gambling, but I was also lucky to experience Dawson City. It was a wonderful and nostalgic place to visit, remote, and not cluttered with tourists. Well worth the side trip.

DAY 5

Leaving Dawson City, I retraced my path back to White-horse via the Klondike Highway. It was cloudy, but dry, so I decided on a leisurely ride. I stopped to inspect a beaver hut on a branch of the Klondike River, eat wild berries in a meadow, and walk in a field of fireweed.

The fire at Fox Lake was much worse than it was the day before. They were halting traffic again and convoying through the burn area with orange pilot trucks (driven by rabbit killers). I waited beside the road for about 20 minutes before the caravan started moving south. When we got rolling, I let myself linger and found a position at the end of the line. My intention was clear. If a photo opportunity presented itself, I was going to drop out of the convoy and take some pictures.

As we started into the burn area, some trees and brush exploded into flames near the edge of the road. The orange pilot truck halted the convoy until the smoke subsided, then we continued to meander through the fire-infested forest. I dropped out of the convoy and took some pictures of a burn area just after entering the fire zone, stopped again about midway through the burn area, and then managed to catch up to the caravan just before the exit checkpoint. The midpoint scene was stark, the devastation complete. From the odometer on my motorcycle, the toe of the fire-affected area we had driven through was 14 miles wide. Based on the burn area I could see, there were several hundred square miles of forest lost to the iridescent red, smoke belching demon.

When I got back to Whitehorse, I strolled around town for a while. My daughter Cristi collects Ty beanie babies and wanted me to try to find one from Canada. I went to several stores and heard essentially the same story every place I went.

"No one in town has any."

"Good luck."

"It's crazy; we can't keep them in stock."

"You might try at _____."

I had no luck anywhere in town.

Oh well, the walk was good exercise. I ate dinner, did my laundry, and then went to sleep.

There was new road tomorrow.

* * * * *

How delicious the taste of a dream lived. The fee seems insignificant while the flavor is alive and dancing on the tongue. The cost is a public stand on what you are going to do, on the dream you are going to live. This price produces commitment in a way that says success is the only option, and allows you to proceed with confidence. This is because we are people with integrity and we must do what we publicly say we are going to do. Taking a public stand on our dream quest strips away limitations we thought existed, and stands us bare before the truth of what we can accomplish.

Positive Action Is The Threshold Of Your Dream

"Far better is it to dare mighty things, to win glorious triumphs, though checkered by failure, than to take rank with those poor spirits who neither enjoy much, nor suffer much, because they live in that gray twilight that knows neither victory nor defeat."

THEODORE ROOSEVELT

"All glory comes from daring to begin."

EUGENE F. WARE

"The secret of getting ahead is getting started. The secret of getting started is breaking your complex overwhelming tasks into small manageable tasks, and then starting on the first one."

MARK TWAIN

DAY 6

My first stop after leaving Whitehorse was for gas, 50 miles down the road, at Jake's Corner. Jake's Corner is at the intersection of the Alaska Highway (Hwy 1) and the Atlin Highway (Hwy 7). The Atlin Highway is a southern route leading through Tagish and Carcross to Skagway. Jake's Corner is an interesting place that sells gas, souvenirs, food, and provides lodging. I met the owner, Dave Gilbert, who was a personable, pleasant, smiling, and energetic fellow in his late 60's or early 70's. The buildings and adjacent grounds were neat and well maintained, but on and around some buildings were densely packed memorabilia of the past, including artifacts from the construction of the Alaska Highway and gold prospecting equipment. The highlight for me was an old flatbed truck parked in front of the lodge that was well-kept and original.

While I was filling my Valkyrie with gas, Dave came over and started machine-gunning me with questions.

"Where are you coming from?"

"Where are you going?"

"Nice motorcycle. What kind is it?"

"Lots of chrome. How much horsepower does the engine have?"

"Is it comfortable to ride?"

"How many gallons does the gas tank hold?"

"How many miles do you get to the gallon?"

"How fast will it go?"

"I really like your motorcycle. How much did it cost?"

Rata tat tat.

I tried to keep up with the conversation but he was on to the next question almost before I finished answering the previous one—an explosive bundle of energy. While paying for the gas I started asking questions about his old truck, which I had been admiring.

"Nice truck, what year is it?" I said.

"I have had several people look at it. Some say it is a 1924. Some say it is a 1926. I think in is closer to a 1924. The only thing everyone can agree on is that it was made in the early 1920's."

"Can I take some pictures?"

"Sure," Dave said.

"Would you like to pose next to your truck?" I asked.

He proudly walked over, struck a half casual lean, half pose sort of stance, and smiled.

"No one has ever asked me to pose with my truck before," Dave said.

"I think it would be great if the proud owner would pose with his truck. That's what makes the picture worthwhile. Otherwise it is just a picture of an old truck."

Dave got a huge charge out of that and his energy jumped a couple of levels. Dave's energy seemed to run normally at a level of 6 on a scale of 1 to 10 and now he was at an 8. He started showing me around the truck, talking about what he was working on now, telling me stories about getting parts for it, and about all the fun he had driving it in parades. He told about what other vintage auto and truck collectors had said about it, then lifted the hood and started talking about the engine. During this time, two customers had driven up to the gas pumps but Dave just ignored them. I was getting nervous about keeping him away from his business, but Dave was busy talking about something he obviously had a lot of passion for, and was content to let the customers wait. After all, they could clearly see he was busy.

"Would you like to trade your truck for my motorcycle—straight across?" I asked, half in jest but half thinking about how much fun it would be to drive the old truck back to Anchorage if he agreed.

"Well?" he said as he rubbed his stubbled chin, "That would be a close trade." Then he smiled and said, "It's tempting, but I think I'll keep the truck."

Then Dave turned and walked over to one of the cars that had been waiting at the gas pump. The car had a man in it about the same age as Dave but more slender and a bit cadaverous. As Dave transitioned from our conversation to his patiently waiting customers, he did not miss a beat, and remained animated and energetic.

"Hi sheriff, you old coot, why the hell didn't you get out of the car and pump your own gas?"

"Maybe it's a good thing you didn't. You look like you're going to fall over dead any day now."

"What do you think about that motorcycle?"

"He's heading down the Al-Can and I don't want you bothering him any. He's a good kid."

"Do you think you could ride that motorcycle?"

I could hear the rata tat tat, mostly one-way conversation continue, as I got on my Valkyrie and rode off. Dave's a great old guy and he obviously loves his life. A lucky person.

Thirty miles east of Jake's Corner, I crossed a high, long bridge over the Teslin River. Once on the other side, the air became saturated with a smoky haze, and remained that way for the next three miles. I could not locate the source of the smoke, no burn areas were visible, but there was obviously a forest fire nearby. The scenery was pristine, but with a fire in a distant valley, the air was thick and irritating like a Los Angeles smog. The road followed Teslin Lake for a third of its length then veered east at the town of Teslin. The name Teslin came from the Tlingit Indian name for the lake—Teslintoo, meaning 'long narrow water.' The lake is 86 miles long, 2 miles wide and has an average depth 194 feet.

Just outside Teslin is the Nisutlin Bay Bridge, which is the longest water span on the Alaskan Highway (1,917 feet). As I approached the bridge, an alarm bell went off in my head. I am not sure if it was the subtle change in the texture of the road, or the color of the bridge surface, or the sound made by an approaching car, but I always listen to my instincts and slowed down. When my tires transitioned from the road to the bridge, my motorcycle began to float and weave. The surface of the bridge was a crisscross metal grating that you could see through to the water below. Narrow metal bars, running the same direction as the bridge, were raised a half-inch higher than the perpendicular cross bars. This made shallow groves the length of the bridge that were slightly narrower than my tires. When my tires passed from one groove to the next, there was a lateral slippage that resulted in a sliding sensation. It was a disquieting feeling. I was glad I had slowed down. At 25 mph, the transition resulted in an unstable moment and an icy road feel, which continued across the entire bridge. Had I been going the speed limit, 45 mph (70 km/hr), I likely would have lost control of my motorcycle. I resolved to watch closely for this hazard as I traveled through Canada. Some time later, I crossed over two creek bridges with the same metal grating construction. I did not like the feeling I got in my stomach when riding over the slick, grooved, steel surface. It was as if I were on the verge of losing control of my motorcycle. From my first experience, I learned the subtle characteristics of this type of surface and the experience allowed me to react quickly, without thought, and avoid a fall when I encountered other bridges made in a similar way. My senses were tuned. A reflexive action was created that allowed me to instinctively respond to the danger signs of this type of road hazard.

* * * * *

Reflexive actions can either help us avoid harm or they can cause us harm. A reflexive action is any action, either innate or learned, that is involuntary. Blinking is an example of an involuntary action. Rapidly applying your motorcycles brakes in response to a danger on the road, is an example of a learned action. Both cases are examples of reflexive actions because they are situations where our actions no longer require thought. The actions are automatic. Reflexive actions can and do save our lives. However, reflexive actions applied generally to different situations can cause us to incorrectly respond in some situations.

In learning to drive a car, you discovered that when entering a curve too fast, you could correct the situation by taking your foot off the gas pedal and lightly applying the brakes. This is the correct response for this situation. In addition, drivers attending professional automobile driving schools learn that if their rear tires lose traction when going through a curve, they are to take their foot off the gas and leave it off. Over time, these actions become reflexive and thought is no longer required.

Transferring reflexive actions from one situation to a similar situation is a common practice. Sometimes this practice works, sometimes it does not work, and sometimes it creates a mental obstacle preventing us from achieving our best. The reflexive actions learned when driving a car, decelerating and braking when entering a curve too fast, does not transfer to motorcycle riding. It is incorrect and can result in an unwanted opportunity to road test your leathers.

If you enter a turn with too much speed while riding a motorcycle, letting off on the gas and braking both have the effect of transferring weight to the front of the motorcycle. The danger here is that this could cause the front tire to slide. When this happens, you no longer have any control of the motorcycle—not a good situation to be in.

The proper approach when riding a motorcycle is to accelerate gently and smoothly through every curve (or at least maintain speed). This is to ensure most of the weight is on kept on the rear tire. Then if you lose traction, it will be the rear tire that slides and you will still have the ability to steer with the front tire.

In the case of how you travel through a curve, the reflexive action learned while driving a car does not translate to motorcycle riding. If the practice is transferred to motorcycling, it becomes a habit that can, and likely will, get you into trouble. Accelerating through a curve, from the perspective of driving a car, may seem foreign and can even be scary, but it is the correct action when riding a motorcycle.

This example illustrates three important points: (1) Braking to slow down in a curve has the potential to either cause injury (when on a motorcycle) or avoid injury (when in a car). (2) Transferring learned responses to similar situations does not always work, so you should constantly question your approach when doing something new or different. (3) Acting in a committed way, accelerating through the curves in the road, is the best approach when riding a motorcycle (and when living a dream) and it is the only way to ensure success.

Just as riding a motorcycle is something new and different compared to driving a car, living a dream is something new and different compared to wishing to live a dream. To live a dream, throw out reflexive actions developed as a spectator and replace them with actions associated with commitment, replace them with actions consistent with moving from spectator status to player status.

There are strong parallels between principles that ensure success in motorcycling and principles that ensure success in living your dreams. Further examining motorcycle riding from this perspective can be useful for showing the importance of questioning the use of reflexive actions in new situations. To ride a motorcycle well and long, there are other reflexive actions to eliminate.

For example, when you drive a motorcycle through deep gravel, sand, or loose dirt, the front wheel on a motorcycle will have a tendency to rapidly oscillate, moving the handlebars alternately to the left and right. The reflexive action is to try to keep the handlebars pointed straight ahead. By doing this, you are aggravating the problem. A motorcycle in motion tends to be very stable because of gyroscopic forces acting on it. Just as the gyroscope you played with as a kid would resist your efforts to turn it, the forces acting on a motorcycle in motion resists course changes. Therefore, when you ride into a section of deep sand and the handlebars begin to move back and forth, the motorcycle is trying to correct the situation. By fighting this action, you make the situation worse by adding energy to the back and forth motion, increasing the intensity of the oscillations. The best thing to do in this case is relax and let the momentum of the bike in motion work to correct itself.

Some of our reflexive actions are not a result of what we have learned but rather come from bad information. An example of this is the commonly given advice about not using the front brake on your motorcycle because it is dangerous. However, when you stop, weight shifts from the back tire to the front tire, so the front is where most of your stopping power comes from. Applying only the back brake will require in a much greater distance to stop then if you used both brakes. It could also cause you to lose traction, further lengthening the stopping distance, and it could set up a potential fall if you don't ride the skid out. (When you begin to skid, the back tire will slide to one side. If you release the brake and suddenly re-establish traction, it could cause the motorcycle to flip. To avoid this problem, when you begin to skid after applying the brakes, you must leave the brakes on and ride the skid out).

This is an example of something we learn and we think is true, but it is false. Transferring reflexive actions from one situation to another situation where it does not apply, and acting from poor or incorrect information are the sorts of things keeping us from maximizing or realizing our full potential. They are roadblocks.

Another thing that can keep us from realizing our full potential is fear. Fear is often an extreme reaction to something we do not understand. Fear, then, is beneficial because it points us toward something that we should come to better understand. Once understood, the thing we fear can become an aid rather than an impediment to success.

On a motorcycle, nervously avoiding the rear tire sliding

while going around a corner is an example of a fear that is much more scary when we do not understand it. Not sliding actually prevents us from pushing the edge of our riding capabilities. Sliding does not mean that you are going to fall. In fact, it is a tool that should be a part of your skill set. If your motorcycle loses a little traction going through a turn, you know you nearly optimized the approach to that turn.

In addition, losing traction can sometimes be better than maintaining traction. If you are going through a turn too fast, sliding helps to reduce speed. Also, when you begin to slide going through a curve, the back end of the motorcycle will start to swing around. When this happens, the front tire automatically turns enough to allow the motorcycle to remain stable. In a situation like this, reflexive actions, like letting off on the gas and braking, could result in immediate traction, standing the motorcycle upright and causing a serious accident.

If you let it, your motorcycle will always try to stabilize itself.

Next, when cornering or changing direction, keep your path as close to the inside of the turn as you can. Then, when you want to go faster through a turn, you will have extra room. This will help develop your full potential as a motorcycle rider. If you run wide just because you can, the mental data bank you build will make it harder to go faster at the next corner because your information says you are near a limit (the edge of the road). Always set stretch goals for yourself. By doing this, your data bank will be filled with information collected while pushing yourself beyond what you think might be possible and will help you to understand your true limits.

Finally, you should clearly know the outcome you want. Do not allow yourself to be confined by reflexive actions or other people's views, know that what you are striving for is possible, take positive action to move down the path, understand that there is no such thing as a problem, and always remember that improvements have no limits so be relaxed and be flexible in your ride. Let your bike take you there.

* * * * *

Shortly after crossing the Nisutlin Bay Bridge, I stopped to enjoy the scenery along the Swift River. This spot was near the Continental Divide. The water in the Swift River flows into Teslin Lake, Teslin River, the Yukon River, and then eventually empties into the Bering Sea on the Western side of Alaska. On the other side of the Divide, rivers drain into the Mackenzie River that empties into the Arctic Ocean nearly due north from where I was standing.

The Cassiar Mountains were visible to the south of me. The next day I would be traveling through this rugged terrain and I noted that the weather looked good. This was going to be the most physical and mentally demanding part of the trip. I began to anticipate the challenge.

I climbed back onto my motorcycle and glided down the road barely touching its surface, the ground below was a misty gray, the birch trees on both sides blurred together like an oil painting wiped sideways with a cloth before the picture was dry, and my motorcycle tilted to forty-five degrees as it attacked the turns. I was constantly scanning the road ahead, and the tree line on both sides. My muscles relaxed but ready. My mind effortlessly defined and then updated the tactical plan for the road ahead, giving me time to feel the wind, to enjoy the scenery, to watch for dangerous situations, and to think again about how to ensure dangers do not paralyze you or prevent you from taking positive action. As I scanned the winding road I was traveling down, I saw a clear analogy between dangers encountered while riding a motorcycle, and dangers encountered in life.

* * * * *

The fantasies we have about danger and the fears these fantasies produce are an enemy of success. When you ride a motorcycle through a curve, you must be fully committed to complete the course of action. Even though it seems contrary to logic and the action produces fear, you must slightly accelerate to maintain optimum traction through a curve. The reason is that accelerating shifts weight to the back wheel, which increases stability and traction. It is actually dangerous to brake or decelerate while riding through a curve, and deciding to stop half way through would result in a wreck.

The same is true in life. When you take a step into the future you want to succeed at, you must be fully committed to seeing it through to the end. To move into the future you must desire the outcome, move deliberately toward it, and continuously accelerate. There is stability in motion, in being in action. Try riding a bicycle at 1 yard per hour, then try riding the bicycle at 5 miles per hour. On a bicycle, the momentum developed when moving forward with commitment adds stability to the ride. Likewise, the momentum you develop by moving toward your dream with commitment adds stability to your journey. Hesitation, reducing your speed, or braking is what destroys dreams. Disaster and failure is in the hesitation, success and safety is in the acceleration. So, once you step onto the path of your dreams, move toward your objective at an ever-increasing pace.

What allows you to accelerate is seeing a positive outcome and knowing it is possible. Seeing a positive outcome is also what motivates you to test your limits, to find the edge of the envelope, and reach for the other side. The keys to success are planning, learning the dynamics of cornering, knowing that it is possible, moving into action, and staying in action. Every time you approach a corner in life, the knowledge from the last experience allows you to move even faster through the next one.

If you allow passion to drench you with experience, the experience will enable you to become better with every ride you take, with every dream you live.

*   *   *   *   *

When I entered Watson Lake, the first thing I noticed was the signpost forest. Hanging signposts at this location was a custom that began during the construction of the Alaskan Highway in 1942 when a homesick GI (Carl Lindley from Danville, Illinois) put up a sign pointing to his hometown. Co-workers and passers-by added to Mr. Lindley's sign and, before anyone knew what had happened, a tradition was born. The City of Watson Lake continues to put up posts and anyone with a sign and hammer is welcome to hang it. At this writing, there were more than 37,000 signs.

The size of the signpost forest was deceptive. To gain a real appreciation for how large this man-made forest was, you had to walk through it. Down every path and around every corner the scenery changed and just when you thought you had seen them all, you rounded a corner and there were still multiple rows of posts stretching into the distance. My favorite signpost was located out side the Northern Lights Centre and showed the distance to all the planets (a spoof—or proof of alien visitations). Surrounding the Sign Post Forest were unique little businesses with intriguing North Country décor. They sold souvenirs, clothes, post cards, ice cream, and barbecued food.

DAY 7

I spent the evening wandering around Watson Lake. The next morning as I packed my motorcycle I began having mixed feelings about riding down the Cassiar Highway. Today was a decisive moment. The many dangers fired at me by others began to ricochet around inside my head—rough roads, fast logging trucks, numerous black bears, many accidents, avoid it at all costs, and dirt roads that turn into bogs when it rains. In the deepest recesses of my mind there was even a thought to skip the Cassiar Highway altogether, but that would sever and lose forever a major portion of my dream. As you come to a curve in the road, the danger is in the stopping or slowing, not in accelerating through it. The fears were not mine; they were other people's fears. To give in to others' fears would be to allow others to decide how I live, to give them control of my life. The only palatable option was to accelerate through the corner, and at that moment, I re-committed myself to traveling the Cassiar Highway.

I finished packing my motorcycle and went to a café for coffee and a muffin. There was a repairman at a large table working on one of the restaurant toasters and I sat down and chatted with him while I ate. As the conversation evolved, I found out he had been down the Cassiar Highway on a motorcycle a couple years earlier.

"You'll hate it because of the rough roads," the repairman said.

He then began to reminisce fondly about his trip down the Cassiar Highway and mentioned, among other things, that I would see many black bears. The clear impression I got was a love-hate feeling—hated the rough roads but loved the experience.

"Do you know if there is gas at Good Hope Lake?" I asked.

"From what I have been hearing Good Hope Lake has gas," the repairman said.

The travel guides I had read indicated that periodically the Good Hope Lake gas station was out of gas. If that happened, the total distance to the next gas station was close to the distance I could go on a tank of gas. Under normal highway conditions, I could make it. However, I was not sure what mileage to expect traveling on rough roads and mountainous terrain, so I decided if there were any question about gas at Good Hope Lake, I would carry an extra 1½ gallons of gas with me to avoid the possibility of becoming stranded.

Even though the repairman's opening line "You'll hate the rough roads," was a bit deflating, the rest of the conversation was positive, and I was looking forward to a great adventure.

After leaving Watson Lake, I had to backtrack 14 miles to

the Cassiar Highway junction (Hwy 37). I filled up at the service station located at the junction.

"Good morning," I said to the attendant as I paid for the gas, "Have you heard if there is gas at Good Hope Lake?"

"Oh, yes," she said, "I try to keep informed about travel on Highway 37 and there has been gas there for the last several days."

"How is the road?"

"There's about 120 miles that's not paved. I understand there is a real bad section south of Dease Lake and the southern end of the highway is very bad—like a washboard. When it rains the dirt sections turn into a bog. Since you're on a motorcycle I would recommend keeping a watch on the weather."

"Appreciate the information. Have a nice day," I said.

"Thanks. It looks like it is going to be nice. Enjoy your motorcycle ride."

With a confirmation there was gasoline at Good Hope Lake, I decided not to take any extra with me. I was relieved because I was not excited about the prospect of carrying gas on the back of my motorcycle. It could be hazardous if the plastic container leaked or if I were in an accident.

Sixteen miles down the Cassiar Highway, I stopped at a picturesque mountain lake with a mirror surface and took a picture to capture the start of this leg of my adventure. This scene repeated itself numerous times along the Cassiar. There were many small to large lakes, either surrounded by trees or in mountain meadows. All were clean and crystal clear. One thing that haunted me as I rode was that there was no one around. No trash, no people in tents, and no RV's on the shores of any of the lakes. Even lakes with recreational facilities such as parking areas, picnic tables, and campsites were vacant. Only occasionally did I meet someone on the road. Cell phones do not work along most of the road, regular phones were rare, and the country, while being reasonable accessible, was desolate. What a wonderful place to really get away from it all.

When I arrived at Good Hope Lake, an Indian village with limited services, I pulled up to the gas pumps in front of a small country store, got off my Valkyrie, and went over to lift the gas hose out of its holder. There was a lock on both gas pumps. My immediate thought was that if they were out of gas I would see if I could buy a gallon from someone in the village. I walked into the store.

"The pumps are locked up and I was wondering if you had any gas," I said to the store clerk.

"The pumps are locked? Just a minute and I'll get the key," she said.

She walked into the back room and returned with some keys.

"We've been out of gas for several days but just got filled up last night. I guess no one unlocked the pumps," the attendant said as we walked out to the pumps.

Hum. So much for all the good information I got. Two sources (the repairman at Watson Lake and the Hwy 37 junction gas station attendant) had told me there had been gas at Good Hope Lake over the past several days, but when I arrived, the opposite was true. Just one more case clearly demonstrating that reality is what you experience everything else is someone else's interpretation of reality, which may or may not be correct, or which may or may not be aligned with how you interpret the same situation or set of facts. If you truly want to know, you must do. You must be in the arena.

As I rode out of Good Hope Lake, there were two mountain sheep in the middle of the road and I stopped and watched them until they ambled off the road and into the forest.

The roads were good until Dease Lake, and then the condition varied from poor, to O.K., to fair, with better roads leading into Iskut. The roadside waterfalls, wild rivers, mirror-like lakes, flower-strewn meadows, nearby mountains, and uncommon solitude for the first 2/3 of the Cassiar Highway was exhilarating, and all well worth putting up with the bad roads.

I decided to stay the night at Tatogga Lake Resort, 10 miles south of the community of Iskut. I could not resist stopping. Liberally covering the front of the tin-roofed log lodge were flowers, flags, and moose antlers. Colorful, unique and inviting. I went into the lodge and inquired about the facilities. The owner said they had sites for RV's and tents, and a few small rustic log cabins without utilities, but located near an outhouse.

"I recommend the Honeymoon Cache," she said, "it's a small cabin built on stilts and has an excellent view of the lake and mountains."

I was hesitant to stay in the "Honeymoon Cache." "Are any other cabins available?"

"There is one other cabin available but it is right next to the gas pumps. The pumps are open from early in the morning until late at night so I am afraid it will be pretty noisy," she said.

"Can I look at them?"

She gave me directions to the two cabins. The first cabin

was next to the gas pumps and across from a repair shop with a sigh that read "Shop Rate $50/hr – If Watching = $55/hr." I agreed with the owner's assessment—not a good place if I were interested in sleeping. Then I went to the other cabin. Honeymoon Cache or not, that was definitely where I was going to stay. It was build 8 to 10 feet off the ground, had wooden stairs leading up to a narrow front porch with two chairs, and the view from the porch was superb. Four log pillars supported the cache, which had rough cut log walls stained a rusty red color; it had white trim, and a corrugated tin roof. The location was also excellent; it was near an outhouse that had a toilet, running water and a pay shower. The inside of the cabin was small, just barely able to contain a queen size bed (with a purple satin bedspread), a night stand, a small Formica top table that looked like it was salvaged from a motor home, a 1960's style chrome and vinyl chair, and a two foot wide closet. The walls were bare rough cut lumber. It had one window in the front and one in the back.

What a great place to spend the night! No longer hesitant, I walked back to the lodge and rented the Honeymoon Cache.

After cleaning up my Valkyrie and myself, I went back to the lodge for dinner. I ordered a T-bone steak with fried onions and a Moosehead beer. As I waited for my meal, I assumed a relaxed position, letting the evening sun warm me through the picture window next to my table. Semiconsciously I peered out the window and watched an occasional traveler stop for gas, a family pull up in an RV and come into the lodge looking for a place to park for the night, and a man on a bicycle ride up to the lodge. I heard some people in the lodge say the bicyclist was from Germany and had been biking around Canada for over a month. Another adventurer, a dreamer, a person in action.

The waitress brought my order and sat it on the table in front of me. There was one plate with hot homemade bread and lots of butter. The other plate, with the steak I ordered on it, had a picturesque country look and tantalizing aroma dripping from it. The baked potato was huge and came with real bacon bits, chives, butter, and sour cream on the side so you could choose how you fixed it. Fried onions smothered the steak. Corn and beans surrounded it. The generous portion of fried onions allowed you to eat a mound with each bite of the steak and there was still plenty to mix with the baked potato. This was country food at its best. If I could lure these people to Anchorage, I was sure a restaurant serving food like this would make a fortune, but then, why would anyone want to leave paradise.

After the best meal of my trip, I went back to the Honeymoon Cache, and sat out on the porch in the sun. I was half writing in my diary, half watching people set up camp below me, and half soaking in the scenery (I was 150% consumed by the moment). While I was writing in my diary, two elderly couples walked up the dirt trail from the campgrounds toward the lodge. One of the women, probably in her 70's, hollered up at me.

"Hey, I wanted to stay in the Honeymoon Cache."

I looked up from my diary and smiled.

"When I saw it, I told my husband I wanted to stay there."

"It's really unique isn't it?" I said.

"Is this your honeymoon?" She said.

"No. This is the only cabin they had left except for the one up by the gas pumps. This one is much nicer though."

"Is your wife up there with you?"

Thirty-two miles outside of Quesnel. Old barn and building typical of this area.

Nineteen miles south of Cache Creek.

Visiting my brother's family in Issaquah.

WALLA WALLA.

My sister, Shauna, helping get my motorcycle ready for a ride.

My sister, Beth; brother-in-law, Joe Hoel; and family.

A family ride.

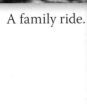

WALLA WALLA TO LAKE LOUISE.

Eroded dirt cliffs.

Radium Hot Springs
area in BC.

Kooteney Valley.

Kooteney River.

Leaving
Kooteney and
entering Banff
National Park,
Victoria.

LAKE LOUISE TO PRINCE GEORGE.

Scenery in the town
of Lake Louise.

Lake Louise.

Hector Lake
and Crowford
Glacier.

LAKE LOUISE TO PRINCE GEORGE.

Reflective Bow Lake.

Mt. Wilson.

LAKE LOUISE TO PRINCE GEORGE.

Ever-changing scenery.

Bridal Veil Falls.

The Athabasca Glacier.

LAKE LOUISE TO PRINCE GEORGE.

Mt. Christie.

Tangle Creek Falls.

Athabasca Falls.

PRINCE GEORGE TO DAWSON CREEK.

Some of Chetwynd's famous chainsaw sculptures.

The Alaska Hotel Café and Dew Drop Inn.

Dawson Creek, mile "0" of the Alaska Highway.

"No." I laughed, "I am riding a motorcycle down to Washington State. She couldn't come with me."

"By yourself? You can't stay in the Honeymoon Cache by yourself."

I smiled at her. There were a few more polite exchanges and the two couples continued up the road toward the lodge.

A little later, another elderly couple walked by and started a similar conversation. I discovered they were members of a group of 15 retired RV owners, from various places in the Lower 48 (a term used by Alaskans to describe the contiguous 48 states), returning from their semi-annual RV trip to Alaska. The group gets together and travels to various places every year, but on even years, they always go to Alaska. After a brief chat, the couple continued along the path.

I leaned back in the chair, closed my eyes, and let the sun warm me as my mind drifted.

* * * * *

I have had several demanding challenges in my life that I have faced and conquered. The more I contemplate the principles of success, the more I am convinced that they are the same for any desire, goal, or objective. Winning an Olympic gold metal, succeeding in business, and riding motorcycles—it does not matter. The success principles apply to any dream you have. You can realize your dream if it is something that is clear and vivid in your mind, if you have a passion for it, if you think radically, if you take a public stand, if you confidently move down the path, if you stay in action, and if you enjoy living your dream.

The key is that you must decide to live your dream rather than just dream. I have been through this cycle many times. Each time with the same positive result. Each time bringing me great happiness and pleasure. I wanted to meet and marry a woman—just like my wife of 32 years. I wanted to raise a wonderful family—just like my three daughters. I wanted to be a research scientist—I have had several inventions patented. I wanted to be an engineer and travel around the world—I have been in 12 countries. I wanted to retire when I was 55—I retired when I was 50½. I wanted to go on an epic motorcycle trip—I have been on one for the last 7 days. This motorcycle trip, like any dream you go after, involved the application of every success principle required to achieve any dream.

I am convinced that all you want, all you are willing to pay the price for, all you are passionate about and believe in, is possible.

DAY 8

It was raining—HARD.

The rain started at midnight with a pitter-patter on the tin roof of the Honeymoon Cache. I remember waking in the middle of the night and thinking it was good that it was raining tonight so tomorrow it would be nice and sunny. The sound of rain on the metal roof was soothing. But as I woke periodically during the rest of the night, it became clear that as morning approached the intensity of the storm was increasing. The pitter-patter increased to a roar of water pellets slamming against the tin roof like a drum roll.

In the morning, I walked down a muddy path to the pay

shower. It cost one Looney (a one-dollar Canadian coin with a Loon on one side) for about one minutes worth of water. Each time the water stopped, which seem to be at the most inopportune moments, I fed another Looney into the slot. After a quick three Looney shower, I packed my Valkyrie in the rain and rode up to the lodge to pay my bill. The couple that owned the lodge was at a table in the back, by the cash register. The wife got up to settle my account. The husband, whom I had met the day before when filling the gas tank on my motorcycle, was reading a newspaper. I chatted with them while I sipped on a cup of coffee the wife had poured for me. They confirmed the worst part of the road was in front of me and that the rain would make some sections boggy. I will never forget the last part of my conversation with them.

"Do you think the road is passable?" I asked, remembering all the stories I had heard about the roads turning into muddy bogs when it rained.

"Just take it as it comes," the husband said.

"You're right," I replied.

Why attempt to define something you have no way of knowing how to define—something based on others' views? While moving toward your dream, "just take it as it comes" is the best advice anyone can give you. It keeps you in action, and does not conjure up any danger stories. "Just take it as it comes."

I thanked them for their hospitality, wished them a great day, and headed down the road. The rain was not bothering me and the roads were good at this time, but I was feeling a little depressed. This was my last day of travel on the Cassiar highway and I had hoped to see some black bears along the way. Bears are prevalent in this part of the country, but I had not yet seen any and was concerned the rain would keep them from moving around and reduce my opportunity for a bear encounter.

Within minutes of thinking about not seeing any bears, I rounded a corner and, as if by magic, right in the middle of the gravel, brush choked road was a sow and her cub. Both were black as coal. The sow was fully mature and looked as though she weighed 300 pounds. The cub appeared to be under a year old. By the time I stopped, the two bears were less than 100 yards away. They both just stood in the road and stared at me. I am sure they thought a Valkyrie on the Cassiar was a strange sight, and I could not believe my luck being able to get so close to black bears in the wild. Yeah! This is what it is all about.

We looked at one another for several minutes. They were content to just stand there and stare at me, but after a while, I started to get bored. Without thinking, I honked my horn with the idea of spooking the bears off the road so I could continue. Instantly, the sow ran to a position between me and the cub, and her expression changed from curious to aggressive. Obviously honking the horn was the wrong thing to do. All three of us just stared at each other—the sow in her new position, the cub now up on its hind legs so it had a clear view, and me wondering if it was possible to quickly become a lot smarter.

Black bears can run up to 30 miles an hour. I estimated that if she charged, the sow could cover the distance between us in about 5 seconds. I decided the best thing to do was turn my motorcycle around and watch the bears facing the other direction so I could rapidly leave if the situation demanded. I did a slow about face on the road and turned in my seat to continue watching the bears. However, my right hand was resting on the throttle so when I turned my body, my hand twisted, feeding a little gas to the engine, and the six exhaust pipes on my motorcycle, now pointing directly at the bears, growled a little—baroooom. The cub startled, and turned to run away so fast that it rolled head over heals ending back on its hind legs a few feet down the road. Cute. The bears gave me one last look and went off into the brush. I turned back around and started down the road. Just as I got to the spot where the bears had disappeared, the sow stuck her head out of the thick undergrowth. I honked my horn as I went passed and she instantly turned head to tail and disappeared back into the brush.

Continuous rain and low hanging clouds prevented me from seeing the scenery along the southern section of the Cassiar Highway, but the ride was loaded with character. Bogs, mud, rain, gravel, potholes, and washboard surfaces all added texture to the experience. It was a fascinating challenge. During the trek, each puddle in the road conspired to cover my Valkyrie and I with mud, and as layer after layer of mud built up, I began to look like I had just finished a grueling motocross race—quite a sight. Parts of the Cassiar Highway were definitely punishing, but even the worst parts were not as bad as I had imagined based on horror stories I had heard and read concerning the Cassiar. Another case that shows you can only know by doing.

People summarize their experiences from different perspectives. Their summary is correct for them but your perspective may be, and probably is, entirely different. This does not imply one perspective is right or wrong—just different. You cannot plan your course of action based on others' perspectives; you must plan the path and the endpoint based on your own views, experiences, and desires. I picked up a lot of fear and many stories of danger about the Cassiar Highway from others. I found the Cassiar section of my trip to be a simply delightful experience with lots of character. I would not have wanted it any other way. If you had been riding with me during this part of the trip, your interpretation of the experience might have been entirely different. I loved it.

* * * * *

In putting together this motorcycle trip, I made a public commitment to do it, developed a plan of action, and then did it. When you are reaching for a dream, you have to be willing to immediately begin moving in that direction. The process is simple—Decide, Plan, Do, Improve.

Deciding to do something and then doing it is the only way to make it happen. Sort out the details while in action. Do not delay starting your journey by trying to deal with every possible obstacle. Most perceived obstacles never materialize, so spending energy considering them is a waste of time and only serves to sidetrack you from your dream. Positive action eliminates perceived obstacles.

Suppose you were riding a motorcycle and decided to improve your cornering ability. What process would you use to accomplish this goal? Simply stated, you would take all the knowledge that you have on cornering, and put it into action. However, as you travel down the road every corner is different from the last, the environment is constantly changing, and it is never possible to know everything because there are too many variables—path, speed, visibility, turn point, road condition, radius of curvature, and motorcycle handling characteristics. In addition, if your objective is to ride on the edge, to maximize your performance through each curve, then a change in one variable will require (or result in) changes to other variables— the path through a curve will define the most effective speed, the visibility in the curve, the best turn point, and the turn radius.

There are always two kinds of knowledge that exists relative to improving your cornering efficiency. The things you know (and things defined by decisions you make) and the things that you do not know. Apply the things you know directly to what you are doing now, and learn about the things you do not know while you are in action. The only way to acquire the knowledge you need to be better than anyone else at consistently riding on the edge through a curve, is to ride through a lot of curves. Only experience will allow you to gain the required knowledge. Experience gets you quickly up the learning curve; abstract analysis has some value but ultimately it is not what allows you to improve; it does not take you further down the path you are traveling, only positive action will do that.

Once you decide, you should next plan, but do not turn the planning process into the goal. This sounds silly but it is a trap people often get stuck in. Are you stuck in the trap? Just ask the simple question, "what are you doing to achieve your dream?" If the answer has any words like planning, studying, analyzing, preparing, evaluating, or scheduling, then you know right away you are not "doing" anything. You are thinking about "doing." As long as you are only thinking about "doing" something you are not "doing" that thing. You are not moving significantly toward your goal. A motorcyclist should be riding, a writer should be writing, an Olympic gymnast should be doing gymnastics, a teacher should be teaching, etc. What is you dream? What are you doing to achieve your dream?

Before going any further, I would like to make it clear that I am a strong believer in planning. A plan is an important framework for helping you to:

* gauge your progress,
* incorporate learnings,
* improve confidence,
* push the limits of what you believe is possible,
* define a time frame for accomplishing your goal.

The point is that if you know exactly how to do something, then a plan has little value except perhaps to gauge your progress and define a time frame for accomplishing your goal. If you have no idea how to do something, a plan also has little value, because as you are moving down the path toward your dream, you will be learning things that will require your plan to be changed. So make a plan that pushes the limits of what you think is possible and incorporates learnings, but keep it clear, simple, concise, flexible, easy to modify while in action, and do not make a project out of the plan.

Planning is both necessary and desirable, but it has negative aspects to it. Avoid planning's potential pitfalls. One we have already discussed—spending too much time planning. Another pitfall is the longer you spend planning, the more likely you will include views and advice from others that does not directly translate to what you wish to accomplish, or does not apply to where you want to go. Working with flawed information means you have a plan steeped in illusion and you will obtain poor results.

Illusion intellectually deceives us. The most common example of an illusion is magic. A beautiful woman steps into a box, the magician closes the box, says some magic words, opens the box, and to our amazement the box is empty. Even if you cannot explain it, you know this is a trick. In our lives, there are illusions that are subtler than a magician's trick. For example, when the moon is rising it appears larger near the horizon than it does when it is overhead, even though both moons are the same size. This is an optical illusion.

Subtle deception also exists in utterances from impeccable sources. Verbal communications do not always allow us to recognize an illusion. We are intellectually deceived because the truth lives in the information but dies in translation of the information to our specific case. We are deceived in the application or generalization of the information. Just like in the moon illusion, perspective hides the truth conveyed by communications. For example, when the owner of the bed and breakfast in Whitehorse told me to avoid the Cassiar highway at all costs, she was speaking the truth but it was from her perspective. When she drove the Cassiar, it was with her husband and children with the intention of quickly going from point A to point B. Because the road was rough, travel was slow, and there were few conveniences along the way, this was a nightmare for her. In my case, I was looking for unspoiled wilderness, hoping for new challenges, not in a hurry, and the fact that there were few conveniences just enhanced the experience. From my perspective, the trip was excellent and I would do it again. Same road, same experiences, but different perspectives completely changed the interpretation of the event—from avoid it at all costs, to do not miss an opportunity to travel down the Cassiar highway. Beware of the illusion of advice, be wary of information interpreted and presented by others. True knowledge is found in positive action and experience, not in thought and contemplation.

The third element of Decide, Plan, Do, and Improve is doing. It is being in action. Action develops experience and understanding which are reservoirs for ideas.

When I first learned to ride a motorcycle, I did it without understanding counter steering. In fact, I did not even realize I was doing it. Steering a motorcycle actually happens backwards from the way you initially think it does. To turn a motorcycle to the left you must push the handlebars to the right. This causes the bike to lean to the left and as you begin to lean, you straighten up your handlebars to maintain the turn. This is counter steering. It is so automatic I never even realized I was doing it until I learned the concept while taking a motorcycle safety class, and then thought about it while riding. It was then I discovered I had been counter steering all my life.

By being in action, I came to understand the principle of counter steering and it allowed me to make large improvements in my riding ability. It may not be important to understand counter steering during a lazy ride down the road; you can do this unconscious of counter steering. However, it is critically important in emergencies and when you want to perfect the art of motorcycle riding.

If you are going around a left hand curve near the centerline and a car suddenly appears from the opposite direction slightly over the centerline, and if you turn the handle bars to the right to avoid a collision, the bike will turn left into the car. To avoid a car to your left, you must push the handlebars to the left (counter-intuitive). This will cause the motorcycle to lean to the right (away from the car). In addition, as long as you continue to push on the handlebars the motorcycle will continue to lean and you will turn sharper. Once you stop pushing, the motorcycle will remain at the lean angle you are at. If you do not understand what you are doing, in a panic you will likely do the wrong thing. Understanding the mechanics of turning a motorcycle not only allows you to improve your riding ability, it can also save your life.

Quit moving through your life in automatic. Challenge everything you do. Like magic, it will produce new opportunities, new perspectives, and you will find significant improvements are possible.

The final element in Decide, Plan, Do, Improve is taking the experience you have had while being action, thinking about what you have learned or what you could do better, and applying it to the next segment of your journey. It is just as important to understand the reason that something works (e.g., counter steering) as it is to understand the reason that something does not work.

It is important to define those things that might slow you down or prevent you from achieving your goal. When you are riding down the road trying to improve your cornering capability, you need to examine your mistakes, and then decide what you need to do to improve your performance. If you just try to go faster, you will end up making the same mistakes at a higher speed. Push your limits from knowledge, not by relying on blind luck. Define what it takes to obtain perfection in what you are seeking, and push the limits of what you think might be possible—you will be surprised by what you can achieve.

Making a mistake is not necessarily bad. It is an opportunity to learn, it is another challenge for you to rise to, it makes you more confident, it improves your ability to overcome problems; it gives you the knowledge you need to be successful.

*   *   *   *   *

There was a slight break in the weather when I reached Meziadin Junction, where the Cassiar Highway meets the access road to the cities of Stewart, British Columbia, and Hyder, Alaska. I pulled into the gas station at the junction. While I was topping off the tank on my Valkyrie, an RV pulled up to the gas pump in front of me. A man got out and began filling the gas-thirsty motor home. Then, a woman stepped around to the back of the RV with a video camera and struck up a conversation with me.

"Can I take a picture of you?" the woman from the RV asked.

I looked at her a bit perplexed, smiled, and said, "Sure you can," while wondering about my instant celebrity status.

"We were following you down the Cassiar Highway." She said continuing to talk as she was filming, "I was taking pictures of you from the back and wanted to get some from the front. I just could not believe you were going down the Cassiar Highway on a motorcycle in all that rain. You deserve a medal or something. Where are you going?"

I laughed while glancing at my motorcycle and my pants that were all covered in mud, then turned to the camera with a huge smile and said, "Yeah I bet I was quite a sight. This is the dirtiest my motorcycle has ever been. I'm from Anchorage, Alaska, and am riding down the Cassiar to Washington State to visit relatives, then I'll return to Anchorage by way of Banff, Jasper, and the Alaska Highway."

"That's incredible," she said, "I still think you deserve some kind of medal or something."

We continued chatting for a while. They were going to spend the night at Hyder, Alaska, 40 miles down a spur road south of the junction. I had not planned to take a side trip down this spur road, but after our conversation, I decided to ride 16 miles toward Hyder to see Bear Glacier, then turn around and continue down the Cassiar Highway. It was a great side trip. Peaks pierced the clouds on both sides of the asphalt road that meandered through the mountainous valley—just the kind of road motorcycles love. I could see turquoise glaciers oozing from between sheer rock walls as I rode. Bear Glacier was not as spectacular as other glaciers I had seen, but the ride through the mountain pass was worth the extra time. I stopped at the glacier viewing area for a while, relaxed on a rock, and got lost in the serenity of the moment, but then consciousness returned and I realized I was wet, tired, and it was getting late, so I headed back to Meziadin Junction and continued my trek down the Cassiar Highway.

I stopped for gas at Kitwanga. The station had a power washer beside it so after filling the gas tank on my Valkyrie, I rode over and parked next to the wash bay which was nothing more than a concrete slab at the end of the service station with a water drain in the middle. I went inside to pay for the gas and see about using the washer. The cost for the power washer was $1.00 a minute. They obviously catered to the mud coated vehicles coming out of the Cassiar Highway and knew most people would pay anything reasonable to shed some of the dirt they had picked up during the journey—and they were right. One of the attendants went outside with me, wrote down the time on the run clock, and turned the power washer on. I was wearing my rain gear. My boots and legs were caked in mud. I thought, "Hell, might as well clean myself off too," and began power washing my legs. About that time, an elderly gentleman, probably in his late 60's, came around the corner, stopped, and was giving me a very curious stare.

"I just rode down the Cassiar and thought I'd clean myself off," I said with a smile.

The old man shook his head up and down for a moment, still not quite sure he was believing what he was seeing, and said, "Good idea." He watched a little longer while I continued to power wash my pants and boots, then turned and walked back around the corner.

The power washer got the worst part of the grime off my motorcycle, transforming it from dull chocolate-milk brown to red, white, and chrome. When my bike looks good, I feel good, and I was ready to ride again.

During my trip down the Cassiar Highway, I asked people at every gas stop if they had ever seen a Valkyrie come down this road before. No one had. To my knowledge, up to that time, no one had ever ridden a Valkyrie on the Cassiar Highway. The fact that I made it down this rugged road without incident says something positive about the versatility of this motorcycle. The Valkyrie is reliable, bursting with power, and smooth as silk on the highway. On rough dirt, rock, mud, and gravel roads, all you do is stand up a little on the pegs and it handles like a dream. It is quite content to take you anywhere you want to go.

Kitwanga was the end of the Cassiar Highway. From here I headed East on the Yellowhead Highway (Hwy 16) to Smithers. Smithers was a pleasant looking town. The architecture of many of the buildings, and the mountains in the background, gave the town a Swiss feel. I had too much cleaning up to do, and I arrived too late for exploring, but the town looked like it would have been a fun place to get lost in for a while.

DAY 9

The road from Smithers to Quesnel wandered through many small picturesque farming communities. Huge square plots of hay and wheat fields, randomly sewn into the forest with thready gray roads, looked like a patchwork quilt covering the rolling valley that was cradled in the bosom of the Hogem Range Mountains and Interior Plateau of British Columbia. The air was crisp and fresh with smells of fresh cut hay, fragrant clover, sweet grass, and pine. It was an ideal road for riding a motorcycle, rolling and weaving as it wandered from one small town to the next, so I just immersed myself in the scenery and enjoyed the ride.

I thought I was out of bear country, but as I crested a hill outside the town of Topley, I saw a large black bear, dead beside the road. It was a recent kill. The back end of the bear was sliced open, exposing red meat, but no ravens or magpies were eating on it yet.

When I drove through the city of Burns Lake, there were floats, fire engines, cars, and bands lined up on the left side of the street getting ready for a parade. The kids on the float waved as I rode past so I waved back—sort of a reverse parade. Hundreds of people were lined up along the main street of the town and they stared, or smiled, or waved as I went past. It felt like the whole town showed up to greet me as I passed through the city. At the end of my trip, I tried to find out about this celebration. There is not a Canadian National holiday on July 11 and none of the other towns I passed through that day were celebrating, so I assume it must have been a local event.

At Prince George, I headed south on Highway 97, the west access route to the Alaska Highway. Shortly after arriving in Quesnel (pronounced Kwe-nel), I passed a Honda dealership. My oil was a little low so I stopped and went into the store to buy a quart. I told the man at the check stand I only needed 3 to 5 ounces and I would be happy for him to have the rest of the quart if he could use it. It turned out I was talking to the owner. He invited me into the shop on the side of his store where he pumped 6 ounces of oil from a 42-gallon drum into an oilcan, and then he said I could just have it. He even came outside and helped hold my motorcycle upright so I could check the oil level while I was filling it. We chatted about my trip while I was pouring oil into my Valkyrie. Afterwards, I tried to pay him for the oil but he would not accept anything for it. I thanked him and waved as I rode off.

Quesnel is a wonderful city located at the confluence of the Quesnel and Fraser rivers. I checked into a hotel near the city center. One of the things I needed to do this evening was wash some clothes. I did not relish the idea of spending time on this task so I just loaded all my white and colored clothes together in one washer, added a box of soap from a vending machine, and inserted enough coins to get it started. I could just see my wife going crazy at this approach to doing laundry, but hey, colored underwear did not seem that much of a problem to me, and I saved a lot of time. I went outside to cleanup my motorcycle while my clothes were washing and drying. After the dust and dirt was wiped off my Valkyrie, I took my clean clothes to my room and packed them. The whites turned slightly gray so they matched the black shirts and pants I wore while riding – worked out better than I thought it might. Then I cleaned myself up a bit and went outside to see what Quesnel was all about.

The motel was across the street from a park located on the river's edge. A walking bridge went from the edge of the park to the other side of a wide river. Next to the bridge was a large wooden water wheel, and adjacent to that was the main part of town containing many interesting shops. In my wanderings, I found a Greek restaurant called The Ulysses. I bought a copy of the local newspaper (the first of my trip) and relaxed with a glass of Boutari (a red Greek wine) while waiting for my order to arrive. The food was outstanding so I savored it with another glass of Boutari then enjoyed the crisp evening air as I walked back to the hotel. A perfect ending to another awesome day.

DAY 10

In the morning I felt good, and decided to challenge myself by driving all the way from Quesnel, BC, to Issaquah, Washington, instead of stopping in Hope, BC, as originally planned.

Issaquah is a bedroom community east of Seattle. This would be the furthest I had ridden my Valkyrie in a single day—500 miles. However, by riding to Issaquah I would have more time the next day to spend with my brothers' wife, Jenny, and their two children Lydia and Afton. My brother Lloyd had recently started a new job in San Antonio and Jenny was finalizing the sale of their house, packing, and getting ready to move to Texas over the next few days. Chances were good that we would not see one another often now that we lived at extreme ends of the United States (San Antonio and Anchorage are 4700 road miles apart), so I wanted to spend as much time as possible the next morning visiting with them.

There were significant changes in climate, vegetation, scenery, and buildings during my trip from Quesnel to Issaquah. Leaving Quesnel it was drizzling rain. The land was mountainous with lush vegetation and forests. Many of the farms had older homes with sections of split rail fences and log barns. Buildings were solid, built to last, and based on the wide mix of architecture they had lasted a long time.

When I went over the summit between the cities of 100 Mile House and Cache Creek, it became hot and dry. The mountains were spotted with pine trees spread thinly among sage and sun-burnt grass. The buildings were constructed with modern materials and were generally newer than those on the other side of the pass, but they had a temporary look to them, and their dreary tattered exteriors made them appear as though they had past their intended life.

From north of Boston Bar to Hope, the road followed the Fraser River, descending through a steep mountain gorge. As the river approached the valley, the forest became lush and green again. The road snaked its way along the side of sheer canyon walls, at times hundreds of feet above the river. Several narrow, two-lane tunnels pierced the granite mountain.

Entering a tunnel at highway speed produced a tingling feeling of trepidation that was the result of an abrupt sensory transition at the tunnel entrance and exit. At one moment there was bright blue sky, a river with steep mountains on both sides, a soft quietness, and the enormous scale of things made the speed I was traveling seem agonizingly slow. Then instantly I was in a dimly lit tube with its surface nearly touching my handlebars, thunder reverberated in my chest, speed was magnified by proximity of the walls, and the small circle of light off in the distance gave the feeling of hurling toward an unknown destination. I felt like a cannon ball. Then instantaneously a transition back into openness and it was almost as if the seconds before never happened.

At one point, the wide river valley narrowed. Steep cliffs rising from both sides choked the river, thunderously funneling water through a spot appropriately named Hells Gate. Not far from here, the canyon slowly folded open and poured into a mountain valley, decorated by the city of Hope.

The section of road between Boston Bar and Hope was such a great ride I would have loved to turn around and do it all over again.

The city of Hope, British Colombia, was located in the transition between the mountains and the plains. In Hope, I filled my motorcycle with gasoline and headed toward Sumas where I planned to cross the border into the United States. When I got to Sumas, the line at the custom's office going into Washington

State stretched for two miles. The stop and go traffic was monotonous but the crossing momentous as the odometer on my Valkyrie turned over to exactly 10,000 miles right on the US-Canadian border.

From south of Hope though southern Canada and northern Washington, the terrain was lush, endless, flat farmland. It was like riding on the surface of a green ocean. The only relief was mountains piercing the distant horizon. As I approached Seattle, it became mountainous again. Then, I was engulfed in the city with nothing but asphalt roads, concrete spires, hurried traffic, and sounds of fury. I enjoyed the stark contrasts experienced during my ride today – still valleys, stern canyons, lush mountains, lifeless hills, damp highlands, dry lowlands, sinuous roads, straight freeways, tiny country homes, towering city offices.

When I arrived in Issaquah I called Jenny, but she was not home so I left a message I would be coming by their house at 8:00 in the morning to take them all to breakfast at their favorite place—IHOPS (the International House of Pancakes). I was not sure where they were or when they would be home, so I found a room in a nearby Motel 6, located right next to the freeway, and turned in for the night.

DAYS 11 – 14

I had a wonderful time visiting with family and friends while in Washington State.

I spent a pleasant and leisurely morning in Issaquah with my sister-in-law Jenny, and her daughters Lydia and Afton. In the afternoon, I rode to Walla Walla in the southeastern corner of Washington State.

My sister Shauna surprised me by coming up from Utah. I have six sisters and one brother. Shauna is the youngest of eight kids. I was nearly 17 when Shauna was born and I left home when she was still a baby, so we never had an opportunity to get to know each other. Since we were both staying at mom and dad's house in Walla Walla, we had a chance to spend some quality time together. This was an unexpected gift that I appreciated. Every morning while I was there, Shauna would help me clean and polish my Valkyrie (a ritual of mine) and we would talk. During the day I took her on rides, we visited, and swam in my parent's pool.

One of my other sisters, Beth, is married and lives about 10 miles from Walla Walla in the little town of Melton Freewater, Oregon. My brother-in-law, Joe Hoel (Beth's husband), is also a motorcycle enthusiast. He has an immaculate candy apple red Honda Magna and, of course, he agreed to take one afternoon while I was in town and do some serious riding. Two days later, Joe, my sister Beth, their son Tyler, and I left mid-morning on a motorcycle road trip. At noon, we stopped in a one-gas-station farm town of Athena for lunch. The café we went to had a shelf over the coffee bar lined with cups, and each cup had the name of an area farmer on it. The locals would just come in, go over to the coffee bar, get their personal cup, pour some coffee, and make themselves at home. It was a laid-back, homey place. After the waitress came to the table to get our order, we went over to a large two-door cooler, got some cold drinks, strolled along the aisles of the half store, half café, took chips and Hostess cupcakes from the shelves, then returned to our table and started nibbling.

When the waitress returned with our lunch, without saying anything, she just noted the drinks, chips, dessert, or whatever else we had at our table, and put it all on the bill with our food order.

After a hearty noontime meal, we rode a 150-mile loop through the mountains, returning to Melton Freewater late that afternoon. The day was sunny and hot and we all managed to get our arms and faces sun burned.

Three of Beth and Joe's four kids were still living at home. Tyler, their youngest son, had a dirt bike that he rode with the same passion he does everything. Todd, their oldest son, had grown a goatee for a summer outdoor theater performance he was in—Guys and Dolls. Dawn, one of their two daughters, was planning a trip to Italy, which I heard later did not work out, but I hope she keeps reaching for her dreams.

One evening before dinner, Beth took me on a motorcycle ride ten miles northeast of Walla Walla to a small country town named Dixie that was snuggled up against the foothills of the Blue Mountains. After passing through town, we turned onto a gravel road that wove its way through fields covered in knee-high grass, and along the edge of forested mountain slopes. The Hoel's are thinking about buying some land on top of a hill that overlooks the entire valley, a place Beth calls "Never Land." When we arrived at "Never Land" the sun was just setting, and the wheat fields in the valley below looked like a shimmering golden ocean that stretched out and touched the horizon. It seemed as though you could see to the end of the earth—a truly inspirational place. It was "Never Land."

On my last evening, I talked my parents into going on a short ride on my motorcycle. They had both ridden a motorcycle, many years ago, but had never been on one as big and comfortable as my Valkyrie. My mom said she enjoyed the ride. After I got my dad back safely to the house, he said, "I guess I'll let you keep it." I assumed from this that he also enjoyed the ride and approved of my toy.

Family is a precious thing and I was glad I had an opportunity to spend time with some of the tribe (an appropriate name for a ten-member family). Since Joni and I have family scattered all over the United States (Alaska, Washington, Oregon, California, Texas, Utah, Colorado, Ohio) we do not get many opportunities to see one another, so we take full advantage of every opportunity.

DAY 15

The evening before beginning the return loop of my journey, mom, dad, Shauna, Beth, Joe, Dawn, Todd, Tyler, and I all had dinner together at my parent's house, and we visited late into the evening. Before heading for home, Joe asked me what time I was leaving in the morning, if I were going to get gas before I left, and which gas station I was planning to stop at. The next morning, when I stopped at a station on the outskirts of Walla Walla to gas up, Joe was waiting for me. Cool. Joe had taken the day off to ride with me as far as Colfax, which was one tank of gas away from Walla Walla. Joe and Beth were thinking about buying another horse, and Joe planned to stop at a few ranches during the return trip to check out some horses that were for sale.

The road between Walla Walla and Colfax staggered through farm, pasture, and wooded country terrain. Our motorcycles reached out and grasped each curve in the road, the tires were barely able to hold traction as we leaned to the left, then to the right, then to the left, endlessly back and forth, leaning, swaying as the road oscillated between east and west, thoughtlessly making its way in a northerly direction. Even though we were on separate motorcycles, we were one in the experience of the ride.

At Colfax, we gassed our motorcycles at a mini-mart, went inside, ordered a latte, and chatted for a while. Outside, we scuffed our heels on the ground, not knowing quite how to say good-bye. We gave each other a big hug, then Joe went back down the road to do some horse trading, and I headed north toward Canada. Joe and I have a lot in common. As we rode off in different directions, I wished we lived closer together so we could hang out more.

This was going to be another long ride. It was 565 miles from Walla Walla to Lake Louise, located in the middle of the Banff National Park in Alberta, Canada, where I planned to spend the night. I had decided to stay off the main highways and just travel the back roads between Walla Walla and the U.S.-Canadian border. The scenery and ever-changing nature of the back roads makes them more fun to ride on than the interstates, and each town, found by the wandering road, was unique and interesting (unseen by tourist eyes). The country roads had countless curves in them, allowing my Valkyrie to spend a good deal of time leaning deeply as I rode through each one of them. I was immersed in the pleasures of the road, immersed in the ecstasy of sunshine filled valleys, and immersed in the charm of the ever-changing hill country that I was soaring through.

Then, as I rode into the city of Spokane, Washington, the rapture of the road condensed into a stewy swarm of industrial parks, trucks, strip malls, and bumper-to-bumper cars. Traffic was heavy, smog bit at my eyes and nose, and as my speed dropped to a crawl, the sun began to bake me in my leathers like a burrito. I unzipped everything that zipped on my leather jacket, to facilitate airflow, but I continued to swelter in the congested traffic, and the sun slowly seared my tortilla shell clothes.

After crossing over into the Idaho panhandle, I was able to increase speed and get comfortable again. I was admiring the scenery around Coeur d'Alene Lake and enjoying the cool shaded freeway as I entered the adjacent national forest. Life was good again. Several minutes later, I noticed a sign showing the miles to Kellogg, Idaho, and Missoula, Montana. I should have headed north at Coeur d'Alene but instead, I spaced out the turn and ended up going 20 miles in the wrong direction. Oh well, life was still good and I had an opportunity to once again enjoy that last 20 miles of great scenery.

Early that afternoon, I crossed the boarder into Canada. The temperature was noticeably cooler (I was definitely back in the north country) and the scenery began to change at a rapid pace, flowing from one theme to another like a video rendition of Stravinsky's primordial sounds in "The Rite of Spring" (Le Sacre Du Printemps). Sixty-foot high mud cliffs, faced with irregular pillars carved by eons of erosion, skirted the road as I climbed one side of a mountain pass. On the other side of the pass was a lush river valley with large green meadows, lakes, pine forests, and distant peaks. Then, as I turned toward Banff at Radium Hot Springs, the melody of scenery transitioned to sheer granite walls close enough to the road to reach out and touch. Streams churned white as they funneled down rock corridors cut by water and time. Then suddenly the gray granite walls I rode through opened up to hundred foot high red cliffs that glowed in the evening sun like a branding iron just pulled from the fire.

As I entered Kootney National Park, there was a jagged mountain range slicing through one edge of the valley. The immense mountains distorted the perception of distance. They looked like they were rising up next to the road, but they were so distant that the trees growing up their side appeared mossy in nature. Trees covered the bottom two-thirds of the peaks, and gray granite peaks poked through the tree line. The entire top of the range looked like a serrated knife-edge piercing the earth's crust from inside the earth.

As I went around one bend, then another, the melody continued its primordial rhythm. There were rounded bald headed mountains, mountain walls with green sides and gray tops, braided riverbeds hundreds of feet wide that cut through a forested valley below the road, and granite fortresses that looked like gigantic medieval castles. The melody continued into early evening, when the setting sun began to play frantic games of hide and seek with light and shadows amongst the rugged ridges and valley floor. The rhythmic beat of the scenery ended in the town of Lake Louise, where I spent the night.

I did not think it could get any better than this. I did not know it at the time, but I was wrong. It was going to get a lot better.

DAY 16

I woke early the next morning surrounded by snow-capped, sheer-walled, granite mountains thrusting themselves abruptly upward here and there through an enormous forested valley. I walked across a bridge spanning a river that ran through the center of the town of Lake Louise, and approached the main business district, which was a small strip shopping center. Among the stores was a bakery-deli were I bought a latte and muffin, then went outside and sat on a bench where I ate a casual breakfast while soaking up the sunshine from a cloudless, deep sapphire blue sky. After lingering long enough to become saturated with the moment but before drifting into total contentment, before losing myself forever following white rabbits through this "Wonderland", I walked back to my Valkyrie, mounted it, and headed toward this city's namesake, Lake Louise.

I rode my motorcycle along a spur road that went up the mountain and ended near the lake. I parked my bike and walked down a path through a patch of woods that opened into a picture postcard. Standing on the shoreline of the lake, the water at my feet was clear enough to allow a perfect view of the rocky bottom. Looking away from my feet, densely forested mountains lined both sides of the lake, and a sheer, treeless, snow-capped granite mountain walled-in the end of the lake. The water's surface transitioned from clear into a perfect mirror, its surface emulated all above it in both detail and color. The water's surface was so smooth and the picture so perfect that if I were suspended upside-down, I would have been content that all was as it should be. I walked to the edge of the lake so I could not see any of the other visitors and stood for a while, as if alone in this postcard world, thinking it could not get any better than this. I was wrong—again.

Driving back down the spur road, I turned north onto highway 93, which runs through the middle of the Banff and Jasper National Parks. All the mountains along the highway were granite with pine trees and shrubbery growing up the base until the denseness of the rock or the sheerness of the cliffs would no longer support plant life. Above the greenery covering the base of the peaks, nude gray granite rock laid fully exposed, sleek, and glistening.

The first thing I noticed was how rapidly the scenery changed as I traveled the road. The scenery was always spectacular and continually revealed new surprises. It was like a visual melody. You could see each note being played with every stroke of the road you covered. There were distant botryoidal granite peaks framed by roadside trees. Then, sheer granite fortress walls rose hundreds or even thousands of feet above the valley. The next beat of the melody brought vertical rock walls lined with tall sculptured pillars like a Grecian temple. Castle structures complete with guard towers were tucked in valley corners. Glaciers spilled like high frothy frozen waterfalls through rock-walled channels. Reflective turquoise lakes formed from snowmelt filled low spots at the base of granite walls thrust from the bowels of the earth. Pyramidal granite structures dwarfed the landscape. Huge monoliths pointed skyward. Severe granite walls stretched tens of miles along a valley. Pulpit towers veered off cliff walls. Glacieral silt braided rivers ran as gray as the sandy beaches they cut through. Waterfall ribbons fell focused by unyielding rock walls. Vertical bedding plains etched tortuously in rock, a history of creation born from enormous and unimaginable forces. The melody was relentlessly exhilarating.

"It could not get better than this," I said to myself, but then concluded, "It's all good."

At the north end of the Banff National Park was Athabasca Falls. The Athabasca River flowed broadly through the valley, and then was abruptly narrowed by quartzite walls. It thunderously dropped more than eighty feet, flowed through an impressive sheer narrow rock gorge, then the river broadened back out and continued its flow as if nothing had happened. An experience unsurpassed in grandeur and raw power by any other waterfall I had seen in the Rocky Mountains.

Lakes, waterfalls, glaciers, animals of all kinds, and huge mountain peaks formed a kaleidoscope of scenes. Each scene was picture-postcard perfect, and the landscape changed dramatically minute by minute. I took 66 pictures, but some landscapes I could not photograph because the scene was too large and too close. Both Jasper and Banff National Parks were exceptionally beautiful. However, as I rode north out of Banff and through Jasper, I could sense a difference. The scenery was still awesome, but it changed at a slower rate.

The panorama on the drive through Banff and Jasper National Parks was so spectacular that I could not find a word to describe it, so I made one up—Grandeuvescent. It is big, up close, spectacular, regal, vibrant, bubbly, and ever changing—Grandeuvescent.

I have been to a dozen countries and most of the states in the United States, but have never seen any place as Grandeuvescent as the Banff and Jasper National Parks. After leaving the city of Jasper, I headed west on the Yellowhead Highway (Hwy 16). It was interesting how the intense scenery I had just ridden through affected my perception. The scenery along the Yellowhead Highway was still beautiful, but unremarkable and common by comparison. The affect was similar to what happens when you look at the sun for a moment then glance away. Everything looks foggy and bland until you recover from the impact the brilliance of the sun has on your eyes.

Riding into Prince George, where I stayed the night before heading north to the Alaska Highway, I noticed the town had a very industrial feel to it. A large pulp mill was one of the first things to greet me on my way into town. Railroad tracks ran parallel to 1st street and lining the street were many industrial service businesses. After the great, wide-open spaces and clean air, Prince George was a stark transition. A similar but opposite transition was something to look forward to in the morning.

DAY 17

When I woke up it was raining, and it rained all day. I headed north on Highway 97. Chetwynd, 188 miles north of Prince George, was a unique community that had earned the title as "Chain Saw Sculpture Capital of the World" because of its excellent collection of chain saw sculptures located around the town, including sculptures of bears, eagles, and a 15 foot tall Paul Bunyan.

When I arrived in Dawson Creek the rain had stopped, but the clouds were low and heavy. It looked like only a short reprieve. The first thing I did was go to the '0' mile marker for the Alaska Highway, located in the city center. Construction started on the Alaska Highway March 1942, shortly after the bombing of Pearl Harbor, and the initial phase of the project ended in October 1942. During the war, the highway seemed to have military significance and the US struck an agreement with the Canadian government to build it. In exchange for the right-of-way, the US would pay for construction of the highway and then turn it over to the Canadian government following the war. Since then, upgrades continually change the character of the Alaska Highway, most of which now bears little resemblance to the original road.

After cleaning up, I rode down Alaska Avenue, a portion of the Alaskan Highway (Hwy97) that goes along the North end of town. I was looking for a grocery store to buy something for dinner. Then suddenly, about half a block in front of me a Royal Canadian Mounted Police officer stepped out into my lane and waved me into a parking lot beside the road. I noticed another officer behind him with a radar gun mounted on a tripod. Speed limits in Canada are in kilometers per hour. While traveling in Canada, I had been mentally converting traffic signs into miles per hour but suddenly had a horrible thought that perhaps I was going 45 miles per hour instead of 45 kilometers per hour (28 miles per hour), the posted speed limit on that section of road. I glanced at my speedometer. It read 30 miles per hour. I wondered if they were going to harass me for going two miles per hour over the speed limit. I pulled into the parking lot, and the officer that waved me in walked over.

"Please shut off your motorcycle and take your helmet off," the officer said.

"Yes sir." I replied, not wishing to aggravate him since I was technically speeding.

I turned the ignition off and while I was removing my helmet the officer said, "Don't worry you weren't speeding. Some kids have been riding motorcycles around town without a valid permit. We are just doing a routine check. Can I see your driver's license please?"

I was relieved it was just a routine check. "Sure," I said.

The officer looked at the license. "Where are you from?"

"Alaska."

"Where are you going?"

"I'm returning to Anchorage from visiting my parents in Washington State."

"Class M1—that's your motorcycle endorsement, right?"

"Yes."

Then the officer standing next to me shouted over to the other officer that was by the radar gun, "American license, class M1 is the motorcycle endorsement, right?"

"Yes. M1 is OK," the other officer replied.

He turned, handed me my license back and said, "Thank you, you can go now."

I asked him if he could direct me to a grocery store. He said the store would be closing in 30 minutes, gave me directions, and I was on my way. When I left the grocery store, it started raining again. The sky opened up, and rivulets of rain fell from it all night long.

DAWSON CREEK TO FORT NELSON.

Walter Wright Pioneer Village
in Dawson Creek.

Marl Brown with his 1926 Model "T"
that he has owned for 58 years.

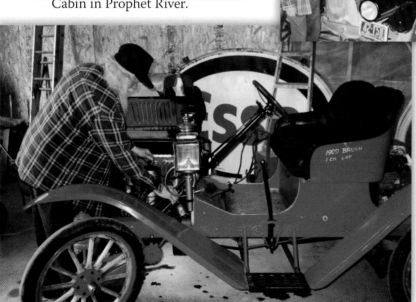

Cabin in Prophet River.

Marl Brown with his 1909 Brush.

DAWSON CREEK TO FORT NELSON.

A trapper's cabin.

Section of wooden culvert.

Old Case tractor.

FT. NELSON TO WHITEHORSE.

Summit Lake, 85 miles outside of Fort Nelson.

Road sheep.

Roadside caribou.

Brown bear encounters are always exciting.

Black bear.

WHITEHORSE TO ANCHORAGE.

Our Lady of Grace
Church in Beaver
Creek, BC.

Gakona
Road-
house.

Matanuska
Glacier.

The journey's end – sky over Anchorage at midnight.

ENJOY THE JOURNEY.

A visit to see Grandma.

Born to be wild.

At Alaska Land in Fairbanks.

Backyard bubble fun.

ENJOY THE JOURNEY.

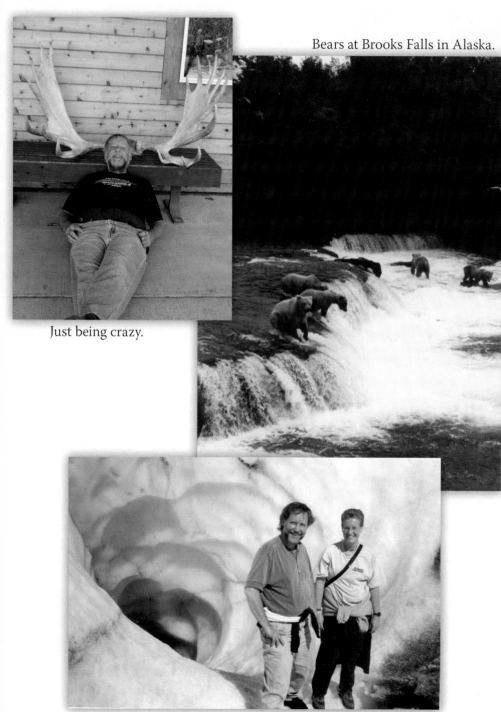

Bears at Brooks Falls in Alaska.

Just being crazy.

Hiking on the Matanuska Glacier.

ENJOY THE JOURNEY.

Kid fighter pilot.

It's a birthday party.

Extreme weather croquet in Anchorage.

Road trip.

ENJOY THE JOURNEY.

Stonehenge.

Stomping grapes in Crete.

RVing – visiting family.

Castle in Wales.

Staying In Action Secures Your Dream

"Follow your dreams; for as you dream, so shall you become."
JAMES ALLEN

"Put all your eggs in ... one basket and - watch that basket!"
MARK TWAIN

"Anything a man can conceive of, anything he can believe in, he can also accomplish."
MARK FISHER

DAY 18

Early the next morning, on my way out of Dawson Creek, I stopped at the Wright Pioneer Village. The village contained an interesting variety of preserved early pioneer homes and town buildings. Some were primitive rough-cut log structures with a natural gray-brown color from years of exposure to the weather. Others were quaint white-washed buildings with thin horizontal wooden slat sides and windows and doors trimmed by flat wooden frames. They were arranged in a picturesque town square setting complete with dirt roads and board

sidewalks. Unique structures like these usually fall into disre-
pair and are eventually torn down to make room for modern
buildings. To save, relocate, and renovate these buildings for
the enjoyment of generations to come was an insightful act that
helped preserve the historic foundation of this city. In Europe,
the benefits derived from preserving the past is obvious. Everywhere you go there are wonderful structures and interesting
artifacts dating back centuries and even millenniums, pleasing
the eye and stimulating the mind.

It is from such foundations that we measure our progress,
growth, humanity, and the worth of what we do, and what we
are as a community. In the United States, preserving the past is
something we are not yet skilled at as a nation. It was delightful to be in a community that understood the importance of
its history, that preserved its history in the form of homes and
buildings and furnishings of representative periods of its past.
The city set aside a place where people can go to experience the
excitement and wonder that comes from a glimpse, a stroll, a
moment in the past. I spent some unrushed time soaking in the
history of this place, then headed north.

The ride from Dawson Creek to Fort Nelson took me through
Charlie Lake, Wonowon, Pink Mountain, Sikanni Chief, and
Trutch. It had been a pleasant, relaxed, and uneventful ride.
Then, thirty miles south of Prophet River (the last small wilderness town before Fort Nelson) as I rode along a straight section
of highway where a hundred yard wide swath of trees and brush
had been cleared from both sides of the road, the relaxed ride
turned tense. Suddenly, at full lope, a mother moose and her
yearling darted out of the trees on my right, ran straight across

the clear cut, and onto the road. As soon as I saw them racing from the tree line, I applied my brakes. They entered the road just in front of me. A picture of me flattened against the side of a prehistoric looking, spindly-legged moose was burning in my brain. I was still braking when I arrived at the point where they had just crossed the highway. By that time, the moose had reached the ditch on the other side of the road, and as I passed, I saw them continue across the clear cut on my left and disappear into the trees on the other side—too close for comfort. I could not believe how fast a moose at full lope could move (much faster than a horse). The road was clear, there were moose in front of me, and the road was clear, all in a matter of seconds.

Whoa. What an adrenaline rush.

When riding, I always keep my eyes open for animals and was surprised how rapidly an emergency developed. Usually, animals along the road are grazing, or standing still, and you see them in plenty of time to react and avoid getting in each other's way. In this case – full lope across the road – things happened fast and there was little time to react. This behavior was not normal. I assumed a bear might have been harassing the young moose, and the mother was taking evasive action.

When I arrived at Fort Nelson, I rode through the middle of town. The towns' people seemed friendly with many smiling faces, glances of curiosity, and looks of amusement cast my way. At the far west end of town, there was a log cabin style museum surrounded by a variety of Canadian historic antiques and memorabilia. What immediately attracted my attention was a blue 1920's "White Moose Bus Lines" bus parked in front, with the door swung open as if it was ready to depart. I am not sure if was the blue bus, the interesting bits and pieces on the grounds, or curiosity about what might be inside the log museum that lured me in. However, the result was that I turned off the road, parked my Valkyrie in the gravel parking lot, and began to drench myself in the local history.

After exploring the inside and outside of the bus, I wandered through the log museum filled with memories and memorabilia covering a broad array of everyday life during the early 1900's. However, it was on the way out that I discovered the most fascinating part of the museum was its curator, a gentleman named Marl Brown. He had a long white cotton candy beard and matching hair that billowed around the top of his flannel shirt. As we chatted, it became evident that one of his passions was antique cars. When he learned I was also interested in old cars, he turned, said, "follow me," and walked toward the entrance. We left the museum, still talking about antique cars. Marl, apparently not concerned about leaving the building unattended, took me to a large warehouse beside the museum where there were nine antique cars—six of which were his.

The first car he went to was sitting near the front of the warehouse. It was a fire engine red horseless buggy with a single black leather bench seat.

"My father bought this car," Marl Brown said. "It's a 1909 Brush, the only car made with both wooden wheels and a wooden axle. It has a one-cylinder, 6 horsepower engine."

"That's amazing." I said, "I imagine it runs pretty rough."

Marl's expression indicated this was exactly the lead-in he was waiting for. "Would you like me to start it up?"

"Sure would," I said, as a grin slowly spread across my face in anticipation of experiencing the awakening of this primitive product of the past.

Mr. Brown briskly walked around to the back of the car, put a jack under the axle, and jacked the rear tires off the ground.

I am not sure the age of Mr. Brown. I would guess he was in his late sixties or early seventies, but he was spry, wiry, animated, and full of life.

Once the back tires of the Brush were elevated, he grabbed an oilcan, squirted some oil into the top of the engine, scurried to the front of the car, and gave the crank dangling from the engine a twirl. It did not start so he grabbed the oilcan again, oiled the engine, scuttled to the front of the car, and spun the crank. A putt-putt and the engine died. It took one more rushing ritualistic dance around the car before it finally started. A putt-aa-putt stutter came from the engine; it did not hum like modern cars. The engine transferred power by a chain drive to the back wheels. The combination of a single cylinder engine and chain drive made the whole car shimmy on the jack.

Now that the Brush was running, Mr. Brown dashed to the side of the car where I was standing, a broad smile cracked across his weathered face, and he re-engaged in the conversation that paused only long enough to breathe life into the 1909 Brush. He talked while the car was sputtering and shaking behind us, frantically trying to free itself from the jack that held the rear end suspended in the air. Marl explained that he had to jack up the rear of the car because otherwise starting it was a two-man operation, one to crank and one to hold the clutch down. Then he began some wonderful reminiscences about when his father purchased the car, its later restoration, and riding it in local parades.

After a while, Mr. Brown shut down the Brush, lowered the rear end, and continued giving me a royal tour. He showed me a 1924 model "T" with the original factory installed carpeting that he had owned for 58 years, a 1926 model "T," a 1942 Dodge model D-23 club coupe that was one of 600 civilian models made, a 1928 Durant, and a 1927 Graham Brothers truck. He was beginning to restore another vehicle recently purchased for him by the museum that was similar to the car he had driven in high school. By his animated movements and the way he talked, he was obviously excited about this project.

Without losing the rhythm of his remembrances or any of the enthusiasm that oozed from him, he took me from the warehouse to a log cabin that had recently been built to resemble an early trapper's cabin. When we got there, he pulled a jumble of keys on a large ring from his pocket, selected one, and unlocked a padlock on the door. Once inside he talked about the process of building the cabin, furnishing it, and tours that had already been there from schools and other local groups. He personally vouched for its authenticity. I had no doubt what he said was true. The ease of his words, the twinkle in his eye, and the excitement in his voice during the stories he told, gave me the distinct impression he directed the creation of the trapper's cabin from his own memories.

After the stories inside the cabin ended, we stepped outside and wandered through a forest of antiques and memorabilia from days long past. For each relic planted around the museum, there was a fascinating story that trickled from Mr. Brown. He showed me an old Case tractor with spiked metal wheels used in the construction of the Alaskan Highway, some early oil exploration equipment, a wooden culvert pipe bound by metal rings that was used in the construction of early roads, and an airplane engine with a bent-tipped, three-blade propeller from a plane that crashed while flying in supplies.

As we walk-talked, we ended up at my still fully loaded motorcycle. He was interested in both my grand journey and my Valkyrie. After several questions, he asked if my motorcycle was very loud. I picked up the hint and started it up; after all, he did start up the Brush for me. This laid the foundation for a parting story about a Harley he owned many years ago, his rides, his adventures, and a crash that ended motorcycle riding for him. Mr. Brown was a fountain of information and after leaving I wondered if anyone had taken the time to write down all Marl knew about the museums accumulations or, if sadly, his encyclopedic knowledge would all be lost when the world loses the treasure of his company.

Later that evening in the hotel lobby where I stayed in Fort Nelson, I found a picture postcard with Marl Brown riding on his 1909 Brush. This was the first time I had ever met someone that was featured on a postcard.

DAY 19

The next morning, while I loaded my Valkyrie in the parking lot of the Fort Nelson motel, a couple from Texas began loading a trailer hitched onto their Gold Wing. I went over to introduce myself and chat. Their names were Mark and Karen. I was interested in how the Wing handled with a trailer in tow. Mark indicated the Gold Wing was heavy enough that he really did not notice the trailer was attached. Mark mentioned they had shipped their bike from San Antonio to Seattle, that they were motorcycling from Seattle to Anchorage, and then planned to ship their bike home and fly from Anchorage to San Antonio. After talking for a few minutes, I wished them all the best, and started up the road.

About 50 miles later, I noticed in my rear view mirror the Gold Wing, pulling the trailer, had caught up with me. On a straight section of road it passed. They were moving—fast! Once they were about three hundred feet ahead, I matched Mark's pace. Mark was an excellent rider, and on normal roads I was comfortable riding behind him. However, along several long gravel and dirt sections where the road was under construction, I found it challenging to keep up with him. While traveling by myself, I had been riding conservatively on unpaved roads. Mark was much less conservative. By following behind, I was able to get a better feel for what my bike could do, and Mark's riding pushed me to ride on the edge for this type of road surface. It was exhilarating.

We stopped for gas near Summit Lake. Summit Lake is the highest point on the Al-Can, with an elevation of 1,295 meters (4,250 feet). After filling his Gold Wing with gas, he pulled over into the shade and slid under the trailer. It had not been handling right and he quickly discovered why. A bracket on the trailer's left suspension was broken. The service station attendant told him that the closest welder was in Watson Lake. Mark decided to stop there for the evening and have the bracket welded, and I said I would stay behind them to Watson Lake, just in case they had any problems. After leaving, I thought Mark would slow down a little since he knew the trailer had a broken bracket, but when we were on the road again, the pace was not detectably different from before the stop. I did not want to travel at that blinding speed so I let them disappear up the road in front of me.

I saw more animals between Fort Nelson and Watson Lake than I saw during any other segments of my trips. The sightings included mountain sheep, moose, caribou, ptarmigan, fox, bears, coyotes, deer, and eagles. The animals were all close to the road, and in some cases on the road.

While riding beside a river that flowed through a rocky canyon, I met a caribou standing on the road. Later I came across two caribou grazing in a nearby meadow. Then, down the road about ten miles, I encountered six caribou walking in the road. I pulled up behind them and slowly followed as they nonchalantly strolled up the road in front of me, behaving as though they were part of the northbound traffic. After a couple of minutes, they crossed over to the other side of the road, stopped, and looked at me. As I started to pass, one of them abruptly turned directly toward me. I thought for a moment it might charge, but it was just curious and seemed content to stare intently as I rolled by. I think it liked the chrome antlers on my motorcycle.

Later I saw a black bear near the tree line a hundred yards off the road. I did not stop; just slowly drove past, looking at him as he gazed back at me.

Down the road a little further was another black bear much closer to the road, so I stopped to watch for a while. It was wandering along the tree line and eating berries that grew in tall grassy patches along the road. It was so focused on feasting that it did not seem to notice me. While I was there, the driver of an

RV traveling in the opposite direction saw me beside the road, stopped, pulled onto the shoulder, and got out to see what I was looking at. A minute later, another RV stopped behind the first one, and then an SUV pulled up behind me. One of the RV owners let their Labrador retriever out and it went running down the road barking. The bear rose up on its hind legs to see what all the commotion was about. It did not appear as though the dog saw the bear and the bear showed little concern for the dog. A minute later, a guy came out of one of the RV's and started yelling at the dog. Things were getting a little crazy for me, and the wilderness I stopped in a few minutes earlier had suddenly gotten congested, so I left.

The next several miles were sprinkled with other animal sightings. On a straightaway, a coyote walked out onto the road, watched me approach, and then continued off into the brush. Along a wooded section of road, there was a doe and a speckled fawn grazing in a small meadow. As I rode by, the fawn startled and ran into the brush, but the doe just stood staring at me until I passed. Rounding another corner there was a fox carrying a ground squirrel in its mouth, prancing toward me on the other side of the road. The fox did not even expend the energy to glance at me as I swooshed past. A moose grazed along the edge of one of the many small lakes that dotted the countryside. Strewn between these wildlife sightings were ptarmigan along the roadside, and eagles soaring in the sky overhead.

As I approached a remote lodge along side the road, I noticed my motorcycles gas tank was half-empty, so I decided to fill up. When I got close to the lodge, I saw a large black bear sunning itself on the gravel pad next to the gas pumps. I stopped on the road and surveyed the situation. I did not see anyone wandering around outside and could not see anyone through the windows of the gas station or the adjacent store. There was a motorcycle parked in front of a nearby cabin all loaded up ready to go, but just sitting there. I thought about my gas situation again, decided I had enough to make it to the next lodge, and continued down the road.

A while later, I approached a section of road with a steep hill that abruptly rose twenty feet in the air, peaked, dropped down slightly, and then flattened out. I glanced at my speedometer—65 miles per hour. As I began the climb, there was a strong "G" force pushing me firmly into the seat of my motorcycle. I opened up the throttle to accelerate all the way up the hill to intensify that feeling of weightlessness when the road dropped away at the top. Just as I crested the hill, a black bear was climbing out of the roadside ditch on my right, and we both arrived at the same part of the road at the same time. The black bear rose up on its hind legs in surprise, twisted to his left side, and took off running away from the road. I got both the weightless feeling I was expecting, and a stomach-churning scare I was not expecting. At the closest point, for a fraction of a second, the bear and I were ten feet apart. A close encounter.

Ninety miles outside Fort Nelson, near the south border of Stone Mountain Provincial Park, there was a sign just before a blind curve in the road that read "Beware of sheep on the road." I leaned my bike over, entered into a tight right hand turn, and just like props in a movie set, as I rounded the corner there were half a dozen sheep in the middle of the road. Whoa! I stood my bike back up, quickly assessed the situation (sheep in the road but no oncoming traffic), then crossed over the left lane, pulled onto a gravel shoulder beside the road, and stopped. The road skirted the side of a cliff with a sheer rock wall on the right side and an abrupt drop on the left. There were some wide spots along the road you could park on, but few guardrails, which made stopping to sightsee or to take photographs precarious. Ahead, cars and campers were pulled over, people were taking pictures, and feeding grapes and apples to some sheep further up the road. I got the distinct impression that people had conditioned the sheep to hang around this section of road for an easy meal, and the sign, "Beware of sheep on the road," just helped reinforce this message by inviting people to stop and fed the sheep.

Sixty-five miles further north was Muncho Lake. Sheer cliffs and water bordered the road beside the lake. On the right side of the road was a vertical rock wall and on the left side the road melted into the lake. The lake had deep blue and green water caused by naturally occurring copper compounds leeching out of the native rock. Along a cliff face adjacent to the road, was a spot where the bedding planes were dramatically contorted. They started horizontal, jutted upward, bent all the way back around, and then continued horizontal again forming a huge horseshoe pattern in the side of the mountain. A spectacular road cut, vividly showing the immense forces that formed the Canadian Rockies.

Fifty miles to the north of Muncho Lake I stopped at Liard Hot Springs. Just off the road, at the hot spring trailhead, was a wonderful provincial park campground. The beginning of the trail from the middle of the campground to the hot springs had a large bear warning sign with do's and don'ts for traveling in bear country. The path consisted of an elevated boardwalk that crossed a torrid marsh, and then meandered through a medieval forest to two large hot springs. It was a pleasant walk. When I reached the first hot spring, there were several people immersed in the steamy water and I noticed a faint hint of sulfur fumes in the air. Surrounding the pool was a lush growth of trees, bushes, and many different plants that thrived in moderate year around temperatures next to the spring, including orchids. The water looked tempting, but I did not have my swimsuit with me so I just enjoyed the scenery, wandered around for a while, then returned to the campgrounds and continued on my way.

On the road outside Watson Lake, I finally caught back up to Mark and Karen on the Goldwing, pulling their crippled trailer. They must have stopped somewhere for lunch. I made several short stops, but when I am motorcycling cross-country, I usually skip lunch and just eat a Power Bar while on the go. We were both traveling at the posted speed limit of 100 kilometers per hour (62.5 miles per hour) when suddenly, a few miles outside Watson Lake (where they were going to get their trailer welded and spend the night), Mark pulled onto the shoulder of the road. I thought this was strange so I pulled over in front of them and walked back to see if everything was all right. Mark and Karen were both wearing open-faced helmets. A bee had hit Karen in the face and stung her. Not a pleasant experience. Mark got some ice out of a cooler in their trailer and Karen placed it on the sting to help reduce the swelling and ease the pain a bit. After Mark assured me they were all right and that they did not need anything, I wished them luck and a pleasant trip, and headed on up the road.

I always ride with a full-face helmet. My friends cover the

spectrum on helmets. Some do not use them unless they ride in a state that requires them (Alaska does not require riders to wear a helmet), some use the minimum (half helmets) and some, like myself, use the full-face helmet. During my trip, I had several rocks thrown up that hit my motorcycle windshield, my helmet, and the visor on my helmet. One rock, the size of a large marble, hit the visor near my left eye. If I had not been wearing a full-face helmet, I am sure I would be blind in one eye now. Instead, the instant after the rock hit, I was enjoying the ride as much as the instant before it hit. Karen only wore a half helmet; now a bee sting ruined her trip (or at least part of her trip). I personally fail to understand why people do not protect their heads from flying objects and potential falls. Today's modern full-face helmets do not have problems with weight, visibility, airflow, or hearing like the older helmets. Enjoying riding, day after day, is more important to me than any pleasure I could possibly get by riding with little or no protective gear. I dress to survive a fall, but wear the highest quality gear so I am also comfortable and can enjoy the ride.

I had planned to spend the night in Watson Lake, but it was early in the afternoon, the weather was great, the adrenaline was flowing, and I had already spent a night there during my trip south, so I headed on to Whitehorse. It was only 580 miles from Fort Nelson to Whitehorse. I also decided to do the next section from Whitehorse to Anchorage the following day, which would be 705 miles. This would be my furthest one-day ride, and I had never had two long rides in a row (+/- 600 miles). The Valkyrie rides so smoothly that a 600-mile day is no more tiring than the rider makes it. I had been on the entire road between Watson

Lake and Anchorage before, so a focused ride, with few stops along the way, would not be a problem. In addition, two long back-to-back rides would test my ability to relax while riding and would force me to use all the cross-country riding knowledge I had learned during this trip. It would be a new personal challenge, and I love to challenge myself.

It seemed like only moments later when I rolled into Whitehorse. I rumbled around the main business district, got a room in a cut-rate strip motel, rubbed the bugs off my motorcycle (seemed especially thick), wandered into a cafe to eat a sandwich, walked around town a little to work the kinks out of my legs, went back to the motel, and faded until consciousness found me again at 5 a.m. the next morning.

DAY 20

This day was going to be a record one-day ride for me—over 700 miles. My plan was to ride aggressively, keep alert, and stay relaxed so I would not get tired. I planned to stop at a few places I had neglected during my ride south, but just long enough to satisfy a curiosity, and shake loose any tightness in my muscles.

The morning was cool, clear, and crisp. The town was barely awake as I mounted my Valkyrie. I gave life to all six of its cylinders, rolled peacefully through the city, moved briskly through the suburbs, and then let the 105 horses I was sitting on loose to stretch their legs along the freeway. The air was electric because of the challenges of today's long distance ride, because today was the final leg of an epic journey, and because a dream that seemed impossible just a few months ago, became possible, and was being savored to the last moment. The day was also filled with triumph and tears, a dream lived and a dream's end, something tenuously here but soon gone. There was an energy in living a dream that had become addictive, and I never wanted to be released from its power. Then I realized, the door only closes when you shut it. Electricity danced in the air. The road jumped up and down, swayed side to side, and the tune it played liquefied time. Now is yesterday and tomorrow. Suddenly, I was hundreds of miles down the road and wondering how I got there.

When time recrystallized, it was two hours after leaving Whitehorse, I was about 15 miles north of Haines Junction, and I had just come up a rise in the road onto a long, flat, straight section of highway. Up ahead was a large brown animal walking down the road about a mile in front of me. At first, I thought it was a horse. I slowed and rode along the shoulder to assess the situation. There was no traffic so my first thought was to cross to the left side of the road and slowly pass. Then, as I continued to approach the animal, something did not look right. It was not a horse. A cow? Hummm, what was it? It turned its head and looked at me. GRIZZLY BEAR. Whoa. I stopped and decided it would be a good idea to rethink my strategy for getting past this animal. I watched for a while as it continued to walk down the road, and then it wandered off on the right side and disappeared into some tall grass. That was a little unsettling because I could not see it, and I did not know for sure what direction it was heading – away from or toward me! After a few moments of intense staring, I saw it again about 20 or 30 feet off the road. I watched it for a while put my motorcycle in gear and started riding up the road. I knew brown bears could run up to 35 miles per hour for short distances, so I kept the motorcycle at 25 mph and in third gear so I could accelerate rapidly if I had to. As I pulled along side of it, the Grizzly took only a fleeting glance in my direction, and then totally disregarded my presence. No concern. No interest. No fear. Of course, if I weighed 800 pounds, had two-inch claws, teeth like nails, and was strong enough to push over a medium sized tree—guess I would not have any fear either. It is rare to see a grizzly bear next to the road like this. What a rush.

I reached Tok, Alaska, at a very reasonable 2:00 pm and pulled into Fast Eddy's Restaurant for a meal that was to be lunch and dinner. I had one of those hamburgers with a little bit of everything in the kitchen on it, extra grease of course, heaps of fries, iced tea, and finished it off with a cherry pie a la mode. Once I was sure I had enough cholesterol to keep my arteries oiled until I got home, I paid the bill, ambled over to my motorcycle, and rolled onto it.

On the way out of Tok, I passed a small espresso shop with a sign that claimed the world's best espresso drinks. I confess an addiction for lattes and was unable to find anyplace in Canada that sold them, so I pulled off the road again, just one mile from Fast Eddy's Restaurant. I am not sure if it was the world's best, or if it was just because I had not had a latte in several days, but it was definitely worth the extra time I spent. The owners also made the whole latte experience pleasant by chatting with their customers as if they were old friends.

Shortly after finally leaving Tok, it started raining, so I pulled into Mentasta Lodge, 47 miles southwest of Tok on the Glenn Highway. I filled my gas tank, but the stop was mostly about putting on my rain gear. While I was there, a man driving a camper pulled up to the gas pump next to me and I asked about the weather. I told him it was clear south of here. He said it had been raining since he left Anchorage that morning and the last 100 miles of road were the worst he had ever been on. There were large gaping cracks in the pavement and lots of construction with long sections of very rough road. I could tell by the strained expression on his face and the broken tone in his voice that he was distressed by the experience. He urged me to be careful. This was not good news. I was planning to be home by 9:00 p.m., but the rain and poor roads over the next 100 miles would slow me down. It looked like these conditions would add a couple of hours to the ride today. This was an unexpected challenge, but I headed down the road to see if things were as bad as the old man thought they were.

I found there were some tricky sections of road over the next 100 miles, but I had seen much worse. Hummm. City folks.

My next stop was at the Gakona Roadhouse for gas. This roadhouse opened in 1905 and was a major stop for stage and wagon travelers between Fairbanks and Valdez. The roadhouse is in the national register of historic places. On the site were a log lodge, the original log carriage house, and several other log structures. Scattered around the grounds was an old wooden freight wagon, wagon wheels, a dog sled, and log hitching posts. There was a pay phone mounted on a telephone poll next to the lodge so I called my Joan and let her know I would be getting in late. My best estimate was that I would arrive in Anchorage between 11:00 p.m. and midnight.

Forty miles further up the road, I started catching glimpses of the Matanuska Glacier. It oozed out of distant mountains and through a black spruce covered valley below. An hour later, I was riding parallel to a part of the glacier that flowed along the valley floor about 20 miles from the mountains where it originated. Even though it was starting to get dark, the slender toe of the glacier that stretched through the valley was a pure luminous white. It seemed to glow like a giant neon light, sharply contrasting the dishwater gray sky and the dull brown, green, gray land. The glacier was spectacular.

I arrived home at midnight. It was summer solstice, so the sky was still twilight. The rain had stopped. Gray billowy clouds covered all but a strip of clear sky in the northern horizon. Brilliant ribbons of pink and silver were stacked upon a brick of blue sky, which filled the gap between overhead clouds and the distant horizon. Above me, a ghostly, circular glow of the sun was visible through the thinning celestial vapors. The moment seemed to be a reflection my inner most feelings. This was a glorious end to an awesome trip and the dawning of a new and wondrous day.

*   *   *   *   *

For me, prior to embarking on this epic motorcycle adventure, and in my situation at that time in my life, the trip that I have now completed appeared to be a significant challenge. There were hundreds of reasons why not to venture onto desolate roads with only a motorcycle and a pack, hundreds of obstacles to overcome, hundreds of scary thoughts, hundreds of easy ways to delay stepping into this particular dream of mine. When I made the commitment to live this dream, my life looked a lot like your life probably looks right now. It was complex, full of never-ending lists of important tasks, and many of the items on the activity list were already past due. In addition, I was married. We had children. I had a demanding job. We had a mortgage, bills to pay, and obligations that consumed every second of every day. So how is it possible to break out of the incessant mire of day-to-day existence and make room to begin to live your dream?

To be somewhere other than where you are today, to achieve your dream, you need only to begin moving in the direction of your dream, to act with passion, to think radically, to make a public stand, to take positive action, to stay in action, and to proceed as though you have already succeeded.

It is a fact that to do, or not to do something, is a choice you make. You may make your choice based on emotion, instinct, fear, obligation, love, logic, or preservation, but it is you who makes the choice, and it is you who acts on the choice that is made. It is unsettling to admit this, because it forces the conclusion that at any moment in your life, you are where you are because of the choices you have made, and because of the actions you have taken based on those choices. It is easy to blame others for not being able to do something, but it is you that makes the choices and takes the subsequent actions. No one else.

One of the most powerful things you can do is to take complete responsibility for your life and the decisions you make, and to admit that you, and only you, are in control of where your life is headed at any instant in time. To believe otherwise is to give your power, to give your freedom of choice, to give your self-determination to someone else. Maintain power over your life, power over the present, and power over your future, by taking full responsibility for your actions and the results of your actions. Do not surrender the power you have over your life to anyone.

Action is the only thing that will begin to move you toward your dream, and your belief in what is possible is the only thing that produces action (to do, you must first believe). In addition, the thing that influences the time it takes to achieve your aspiration is a focused and clear action plan. Focused actions consist of a clear view of the steps required to reach your desired end point, and challenging metrics that define how and when you wish to achieve your goal. Your metrics should stretch you beyond the limit of what you believe is possible because, as your move into action, you will surprise yourself with what you can actually accomplish. If you believe in your dream quest and take actions toward living your dream that are focused, clear, and challenging, and if you stay in action, you will succeed.

Once you start to live your dream, staying in action is vital because slowing, stopping, and turning around are all death-blows to success. Action results in experience and understanding, and experience and understanding are reservoirs for ideas that allow you to sustain action – a virtuous circle. So, how do you remain in action after you start toward your dream? Four powerful tools include: (1) maintaining focus, (2) setting challenging goals, (3) making improvements, and (4) knowing that you are the world's expert in matters relating to your dream.

To stay in action you must maintain focus and eliminate distractions. This attribute will allow you to quickly move down the path of your passion. It is spending time on all the little things that have small impacts on achieving your dream that causes you to slow, stop and turn away. Confront the stuff that slows your progress—problems, lack of understanding, the long list of things you think you must do first, and the perceived monsters that are about to leap out and consume you. However, do not slow down. Grow as you go. While remaining in action; define explicitly what you need to do to continue moving forward; read or talk to experts to fill knowledge gaps; look at your to do list and ask, "How is this helping to achieve my dream?" and "What would happen if I did not do it?" then cross it off your list if it does not significantly impact your progress; as for the monsters, ask yourself what is the worst thing the monsters could do to you, reconcile yourself to that, adopt mitigative measures, and keep stepping steadily toward your dream.

To stay in action you must also set challenging goals. This will help you stay focused on your dream. Set goals, but look at them as ways to challenge you on your journey, not as targets but as something that is hurling you toward your dream, as a foundation to be improved upon, as an opportunity to find a way to get you there faster. By telling yourself that you will move to the next step of your plan in half the time you believe might be possible, you will find that new and exciting doors will be opened to you and opportunities will come to light that you did not know existed. Try it!

Challenging yourself to get to the next step in half the time you believe might be possible (or to achieve twice as much as you believe might be possible) is a powerful tool, because it allows you to take a different perspective on the challenge you are facing. Taking a different perspective enables you to see new and exciting ways to address the challenge.

For example, if I were to say to you imagine a bicycle that can go 5 miles per hour on a road. You would see clearly a picture of a standard bike. If I were to say to you, imagine a bicycle that could go 20 miles per hour. You would see clearly a 10 or 15 speed bike. If I were to say to you, imagine a bicycle that could go 100 miles per hour. You would see clearly a motorcycle. If I were to say to you, imagine a bicycle that could go 300 miles per hour. You would see clearly a jet engine powered bike. Chances are that when asked to imagine a bicycle that can go 5 miles per hour, you did not see a bicycle with multiple gears, a motor, or a jet engine. When imagining a bicycle that could go 5 miles per hour, your perspective determined the whole world of what a bicycle could be, and closed you off from what might be possible. Even now, following this simple exercise, you probably have not imagined what a 1,000 mile per hour bicycle might look like.

It is not that the technologies do not exist. In each case, the technology to make a bike that will go 5 miles per hour, 20 miles per hour, 100 miles per hour, 300 miles per hour, and 1000 miles per hour already exists. The problem is that when we are focused on the 5 miles per hour bike, then none of the other possibilities influence our thinking. When we think about increasing the speed of a bicycle from a 5 miles per hour perspective, we think in terms of the 5 miles per hour bike design. This would lead us to design changes like graphite grease on the bearings, narrow high-pressure tires, light alloys, and aerodynamics. All the improvements we think of from the 5 miles per hour bike perspective have insignificant impacts compared to the impact of adding gears, and the impact of adding gears is insignificant when compared to the impact of adding a motor, and the impact of adding a motor is insignificant when compared to the impact of adding a jet engine. The same is true when you tell yourself that you want to accomplish something in a certain amount of time. For example, "I want to retire when I am 65." At the instant you define 65 as your goal, you have fixed your perspective, and the course of action you take will be aligned with that perspective. When you change your perspective, "I want to retire when I am 55," you are able to see new pathways for reaching out and achieving your dream. Do not limit yourself to a 5 miles per hour bicycle. When stepping toward your dreams, take the 1000 mile per hour bike perspective.

In addition, to stay in action you must observe what you are doing, be open to experimentation, and find ways to make improvements. You can only consistently improve future results by changing what you did, not by speculating about what you should have done. A common mistake in analyzing something that has happened is to say, "I should have done X Y Z." Thinking in terms of "should haves" is not productive and leaves you with nothing to change. In contrast, consistent improvement comes from a considered action plan. An "I will" approach instead of an "I should have" approach. This is a subtle but extremely important point.

For example, if I take my favorite motorcycle ride along a winding country road with the objective of riding on the edge, and if my back tire slides a little when I go through a particular curve in the road, then I might think something like, "I should have gone slower through that curve." There are two problems with this approach. First, the "should have" approach does not leave you with a specific action for improving your performance the next time you push yourself through a similar curve, and second, it avoids the problem rather then finding the solution. The best tactic is to look objectively at what you did, and then define a corrective action based upon what you did, and actions you can take next time. By analysis, you might find your speed was O.K. but your turn point was late. This would lead you to think something like, "Next time I will maintain my speed through this turn but begin my turn earlier and use all of the road as I go through the curve instead of hugging the inside of the lane." With the latter methodology, you learned from what you specifically did, you have defined a way to improve your performance the next time you go through a similar curve, and you have corrected a mistake in your riding technique. The second problem mentioned regarding using the "should have" approach (avoiding the problem rather than finding the solution) is that the speculative solution of "going slower" just allows you to make the same mistake without experiencing the consequences of your poor riding practices (back tire sliding as you go through the curve). This keeps you from growing.

To make changes, look at what happened and what you can do differently. It is the difference between being haphazard and random, or being specific and methodical. This is the key to improvement. A mistake is a result of a specific action taken, so look at the action taken and decide on an action to specifically resolve the mistake. Do not randomly take another approach hoping the problem will disappear; this approach may actually make the problem worse and will keep you from reaching your full potential. The "I will" approach allows you to consistently ride on the edge and continually improve.

Finally, to stay in action you must listen to advice given, extract anything useful, and ignore all the rest. Since you are the one on this journey toward your dream, you are your own best advisor because you are the one doing it, and because of that, you are the world's expert on where you are now, and what is required to get to where you want to be. No one else has better information than you on what you have experienced to date, and what you need to do next. Even if the advice that is given is 100% correct, it is only 100% correct for the situation from which the information was extracted, and from the point of view of the person giving the advice. However, the advice may not apply to your situation or the direction you are heading. In the final analysis, you are the only one that can decide how to move down the road you are traveling.

Where would we be if we acted on others' views? Here are a few statements of fact that when ignored, changed the world: Fact, the earth is flat and if you sail to far from shore you will fall off the edge; Fact, the sun, moon and stars revolve around the earth; Fact, man can't fly; Fact, it will take a century to put a man on the moon. While these statements contained the best knowledge available at the time, they seem silly to us today. In retrospect, you will find that seemingly sound advice received from well-wishers regarding your dream quest is just as silly, and makes just as little sense relative to your journey.

Never think you are not doing well or you are unable to do something because of someone else. There is not someone else between you and your dream. Only you. Show no fear and keep moving. It is what you do that makes things happen.

Succeeding at your dream is a lot like riding a motorcycle.

Keeping the throttle on, while perhaps contrary to reflexive actions, is the best way to maintain stability through the curves in the road. Motorcycles are more stable when they are accelerating—so are people.

There are only two types of people in the world, those who believe everything is possible, and those who believe only what they believe possible, is possible. The only difference between these two groups is the first group chooses not to limit themselves. Which group are you in?

Remember. To experience the richness of your dreams you have to feel it, you have to do it, you have to live it, and you have to stay in action.

Enjoying The Journey

"Winners expect to win in advance. Life is a self-fulfilling prophecy."

UNKNOWN

"For a long time it had seemed to me that life was about to begin - real life. But there was always some obstacle in the way, something to be got though first, some unfinished business, time still to be served, a debt to be paid - then life would begin. At last it dawned on me that these obstacles were my life."

ALFRED D'SOUZA

"It's not the thing we do we regret, It's the things we've never done."

SAUL ALINSKY

"If you can dream it, you can do it."

ROBERT H. SCHULLER

This story merges principle with practice while showing how glorious it is to live your dream, instead of just dreaming. Through the story, you discovered the principles that will allow you to live your dreams, and at the same time, you vicariously experienced the grandeur associated with living a dream by reading about a dream I lived.

The story is about my dream of motorcycles and a journey along the edge of a wilderness. The dream, when realized, was laced with unimagined joys, dripped with challenge and adventure, and fizzed with life, and I lingered in it. I discovered that once I indulged myself, once I allowed myself to live a dream, it transformed the way I existed, it transformed the way I related to the world around me, and I could not recede back into the cave of my previous existence. It was an evolutionary step.

During the journey, I constantly searched for limits. I found the top speed of my motorcycle was 138 miles per hour, when cornering it could lean until the foot peg scraped on the ground, and it could accelerate from a stop rapidly enough to raise the front tire off the ground. While I found the limits of my Valkyrie, I could not find my limits, but I continue to search, to probe, and to seek, even though it may take a lifetime. It is a search I will never tire of, because I never feel more alive than when I am living on the edge, when I am stepping toward realizing my full potential.

When I returned from this trip, I made a life changing decision. I quit my job of 18 years and my profession of 26 years, and decided to walk only down the paths of my dream quests. I decided to earn my living, spend my time, and expend my energies consistent with my dreams. No longer would my dreams be relegated to the future. Any path you choose to take has risks, hardships, disappointments, rewards, excitement, joy, enchantments, and exhilarations. The road toward your dream quest is no more hazardous, and no more uncertain than any other road you select. So why walk down a road other than the one you wish to be on? Why trade a dream for a mere existence? There is no gain. There is great loss.

There are many things I have wanted and achieved in life: a new car, college education, wife, children, house, and career. These are all aspirations, things born from desire, from need, and from love. However, a dream is born of passion, and a vibrant life is conceived by swirling aspiration and dream, by splashing the two together. Vibrance is felt by the vigor, the excitement, the daily renewal, the act of throwing yourself out of bed and racing toward your day, embracing it, and being energized by it. If vibrance is missing for you, sprinkle your dream quest into your life, and feel life begin to effervesce.

The Journey, any journey you choose to take, is your life. What you do, is how you choose to live your life. This book points towards a process for choosing your dreams as the path you take, and how to have fun while on the journey. The quest of your dream is about challenge, discovery, and having an exhilarating experience. However, as you travel, always remember what is important, and maintain a positive interaction with your family and friends, because in the final analysis, when the sky is bright or dark, they are the things of greatest value, they are what make it all worthwhile. Remain focused on why you are taking the journey, and maintain a balance between family, friends, health, socialization, learning, community, diverse experiences, country, God, and your dream quests. It is all the ingredients in apple pie that makes it so delicious. You can never replicate the experience of eating an apple pie by separately tasting each of the ingredients. You have to mix all the ingredients together and then taste.

What you do with every now, decides your tomorrow. Take control, relax, and enjoy the ride. Make your life an adventure and experience the freedom, the wind, and success.

The Dream I Am Going to Live

MY DREAM (what am I passionate about, can see vividly in my mind, and can feel the joy of living? I will be living this dream by this date:_____
My dream stretches the limits of what I think is possible, but it's worth my efforts.):

PRINCIPLES (guiding principles that will make my dream happen):

ACTIONS (what I need to do to start living my dream now):

Email comments to: liveyourdreamsnow@edenscapepublishing.com